Performance Management
REBOOT

ENDORSEMENTS

We all know that the heart of productivity and sustainable profitability is equatable to the collective performance of every employee. In the midst of raging debates on ditching performance management ratings and what to replace them with, and what this might mean for bonuses, increases, promotions, engagement and EVP, this book provides the freshest empirical research, guidance, practical tools, tips and expert advice on performance management in the new world of work with no bamboozling jargon.

This book challenges conventional wisdom on performance management and helps us redefine how employees might more constructively experience performance management. The book will enable us to better understand how continuous feedback, collaborative goal-setting, and ongoing coaching can help to produce business results. This book also helps us to move from disparaging, anxiety-driven engagements and painful, time-consuming administration, to powerfully enabling people to be the best they can be.

Professor Shirley Zinn, Group Head of Human Resources,
Woolworths Holdings Ltd; and bestselling author of 'Swimming Upstream'

In this book Dr Bussin shows that the hype about the death of performance management has proven to be without substance. Whilst the discipline of performance management is constantly evolving as organisations attempt to adapt to a changing environment, the basic principles of performance management remain as relevant today as ever before.

Xolani Mhlaluka, Senior Executive – Human Resources, SAICA

First published in 2017

ISBN: 978-1-86922-664-0
eISBN: 978-1-86922-665-7 (ePDF)

Published by KR Publishing
P O Box 3954
Randburg
2125
Republic of South Africa

Tel: (011) 706-6009
Fax: (011) 706-1127
E-mail: orders@knowres.co.za
Website: www.kr.co.za

Printed and bound: HartWood Digital Printing, 243 Alexandra Avenue, Halfway House, Midrand
Typesetting, layout and design: Cia Joubert, cia@knowres.co.za
Cover design: Cia Joubert, cia@knowres.co.za
Editing & proofreading: Valda Strauss, valda@global.co.za
Project management: Cia Joubert, cia@knowres.co.za
Index created with TExtract / www.Texyz.com

Performance Management REBOOT

Fresh perspectives for the changing world of work

A practical and informative textbook for managing performance for the changing world of work

Dr Mark Bussin

2017

TABLE OF CONTENTS

ACKNOWLEDGEMENTS

This book would not have been published without the contributions from many very dedicated people – thank you for sharing your expertise.

Thank you to the authors of, and contributors to, the relevant chapters and Daniela Christos for all the help and inputs.

Many more of my colleagues have inspired me and challenged my thinking – thank you to you all.

To Knowledge Resources, thank you for coordinating the production and marketing of this book.

A special thank you to Chris Blair for his insight and for allowing me to do what I enjoy – writing and teaching.

A giant thank you to Marina, Daniel, Kate, Genna and James for your inspiration and patience.

To you, the reader, I look forward to receiving your inputs and to building on the experiences that you have had with performance management and your suggestions as to how we can improve our knowledge and practice in this relatively poorly practised field of management.

Dr Mark Bussin
Johannesburg, 2017

drbussin@mweb.co.za
www.drbussin.com
+27 82 901 0055

FOREWORD

This book, amongst other things, reflects the professional journey the writer has undertaken, a journey he has unselfishly decided to share with business colleagues, scholars and everyone interested in the subject of performance management. The book is built on the premise that, in life, as in business, nothing is static, and, therefore, time and again interrogation of the efficacies of current management practices in relation to the associated return-on-investment realities is key.

This author's natural approach, which is informed by his deep empirical and practical exposure in business and strategic HR in general, flows from a systems and holistic view of management performance as an ideal operating model – to the extent that performance management as an HR tool alone would be completely amorphous if not included in the overall HR strategy. Admittedly, it is one of the pivotal and enabling building blocks in the total rewards approach. More pertinently, however, the identification of performance strengths and gaps at business value-chain, employee and organisational level enables sustainable performance solution orientation to take effect.

To whet your appetite, let me hasten to say that this book is, in summary, a distillation of the latest tools, research findings and expert opinion on the subject matter. A comprehensive, balanced approach has been negotiated for it not to be too academic, and, most importantly, easy to read and practical for consumption by all interested parties.

Let me say categorically that there is no better time than now to have a book of this nature when business in the world of work is grappling with performance issues. While we recognise that complicated business issues have some bearing on this, we cannot ignore the endless opportunities to reinvent existing business models. This does not in any way underplay the role of individual productivity to improve business performance. Now is the time to elevate our game plan for performance management, and, to a great degree, this book will effectively contribute to equipping all those with a lifelong learning ethic to be better prepared and to refocus.

Mawethu Cawe
Past Group Executive: HR & Transformation and successful farmer
Avusa Limited – Leading Media and Entertainment Company

ABOUT THE AUTHOR

Mark is the Chairperson of 21st Century, a specialist reward consultancy. He has reward experience with many multinational companies across all industry sectors, and is viewed as a thought leader in the HR, remuneration and performance arena. He serves on, and advises, numerous boards, remuneration and audit committees on executive remuneration, strategy and board performance.

Mark holds a Doctorate of Commerce. He has published or presented over 400 articles and papers. He has appeared on television and radio, and in the press, giving expert views on remuneration, performance related pay and management. Mark is a guest lecturer at several universities and supervises masters' dissertations and doctoral theses in the reward area. He is the past President of SARA (South African Reward Association) and past Commissioner for the Remuneration of Public Office Bearers in the Presidency. In his spare time, he likes flying Cessnas and spending time with his family.

SOURCING OF FIGURES AND DIAGRAMS

Many of the figures and diagrams used in this publication have been accumulated over a 35-year consulting and development history by several people executive and developmental practitioners. The following is a guide to key sources:

21ˢᵗ Century: from the files and archives of 21ˢᵗ Century (Pty) Ltd.

Cook: from the work of Gary Cook, Director of Valuemetrics, an organisation specialising in enabling the performance-driven enterprise. Gary is an applied manufacturer of customised dashboards and leader boards. He creates and customises dashboards for the competitive war rooms of blue-chip organisations around the country.

Huss: from the work of Arvid Huss, people professional and applied behavioural scientist. Many of the figures were initially conceptualised by Arvid during his extensive management consulting career; and many of these have also been drawn up from first principles, using proprietary Microsoft PowerPoint© software of the time.

Other sources are individually acknowledged.

LIST OF CONTRIBUTORS

The following contributors are true experts and have developed world-class methodologies in performance management and related fields. They are thought leaders who are highly regarded by peers and clients alike.

Chris Blair, Chief Executive Officer, 21st Century
cblair@21century.co.za

Ntombizone Feni, Executive Director, 21st Century
nfeni@21century.co.za

Reone Kerr, General Manager Western Cape, 21st Century
rkerr@21century.co.za

Ian McGorian, Executive Director, 21st Century
imcgorian@21century.co.za

Bryden Morton, Executive Director, 21st Century
bmorton@21century.co.za

Morag Phillips, Executive Director, 21st Century
mphillips@21century.co.za

Craig Raath, Executive Director, 21st Century
craath@21century.co.za

Dr Ronel Nienaber, VP: Global Rewards and Benefits, Sasol
ronel.nienaber@sasol.com

Debbie Craig
Catalyst Consulting (Pty) Ltd, Managing Director
debbie@catalystconsulting.co.za

John Gatherer
Catalyst Consulting (Pty) Ltd, Chief Operating Officer
john@catalystconsulting.co.za

PROLOGUE

The media seems to be in a frenzy with provocative and seductive headlines like – time to kill performance ratings, or how company X threw out performance management! I say seductive, because line managers who don't like doing performance management (PM) hung on to this notion for dear life. They bombarded the HR folk with emails showing how many organisations are "ditching" performance ratings and performance management. The HR folk in turn connected with me and commissioned extensive research into this. The primary questions were – who has ditched PM and what did they replace it with? The secondary questions were – how do they now give pay increases and bonuses?

After an extensive search, I couldn't find any organisations who had ditched it completely. Yes, many organisations were simplifying and streamlining, but none were ditching it. I then expressly set up interviews with a senior leader from each organisation listed in the media and privately. I was told that those media articles were a little too sensationalist. A primary purpose of this book is to share some of the new best practices and ideas.

I have been talking at conferences and lecturing to thousands of people for several years. Whenever the opportunity presents itself, I can't resist asking the audience just one question:

> "Who here can say that they have an excellent performance management system
> in their company, and that it is working well and folk think it is fair?"

This book is inspired by the 99 per cent of people who did **not** put their hands up. I started wondering why there were so many people who thought that there was no successful performance management system. I have been lecturing in performance management for several years and many pass the course. They understood the concept and how to implement it. There are thousands of books and gurus on the subject. Yet, there are so few examples of where it is practised well. Why, I ask myself? What is missing? Everyone knows what performance management is, have read the books, have heard the gurus, yet there are so few outstanding success stories.

The second reason that inspired me to write this book is a philosophical question I have been asking myself for years. I have children and I praise and guide them like most other parents do. I hope that we have raised them well, and that, God willing, they will lead happy and successful lives. I wonder if this whole cycle is, broadly speaking, similar to performance management. It is not an event, but a continuous process – the way our family does things.

When they do well, I praise them straight away. I don't wait for a week or a month to pass. Similarly, when they need guidance, I give it almost immediately. I don't wait for a few weeks to go by. I give it in a positive and nurturing way. If they need extra lessons, we arrange for these. There aren't elaborate forms and plenty of pieces of paper to fill in. I wonder how similar this is to performance appraisal? We all do it in our homes almost every day with our children, family members, the house help, the garden service, the plumber and any other service provider.

Why, then, when we get to work, don't we know what it is or how to do it? Are there lessons to be learnt from this, and is there any empirical evidence (scholarly research) to support this?

Well, there is!

This book is different for the following reasons:

1   It is based on years of personal experience in implementing hundreds of performance management systems in companies.
2   Contributors to the book have actually done and experienced what they are writing about.
3   It is underpinned by empirical research.
4   It is practical and, for once, tells you how to do it, with no missing steps or information. There are tool kits, forms and check lists that can be used instantly.
5   It is written in plain English with no bamboozling jargon, with many practical examples and templates that you can amend to suit your needs.
6   If you feel that clarification is required, my contact details are supplied. I am not this black hole that no one knows how to approach.

A final reason why this book is different is that it includes practical examples of different types of performance appraisal methodologies, namely the

•   Outputs Approach
•   Traditional Approach
•   Balanced Scorecard
•   Multirater/360°

I am confident that you will be able to design, implement and use a performance management system that is perceived as fair by all stakeholders and which stimulates better performance. I look forward to hearing from you or reading about your successes!

1   INTRODUCTION AND CONTEXT

1.1. INTRODUCTION

Managing a business is even more demanding when market conditions are tough or uncertain. Planning can be difficult when your business, its customers and suppliers are faced with rising prices, falling sales, shrinking margins, and cash flow problems. Redundancies and business failures further diminish market confidence. Together with increasing international competition, tough economic conditions often lead to businesses having to do more with less. The balance between efficiency and sustainability is a delicate one. Cutting costs can endanger future sustainability and contribute to employee burnout and loss of morale.

In order to get this balance right, organisations are increasingly focusing on performance management. All organisations do performance management – formally or informally. And there are a plethora of theories, methods and tools that can be used – some more successfully than others. But that is the point – there is no "one-size-fits-all". What works in a firm of attorneys may not necessarily work in a construction company. Also, it may be a generation issue. What worked with "Baby Boomers", may no longer work with the "Generation Y", as their priorities and motivational factors are vastly different. These are some of the reasons why the field is constantly evolving. Some old techniques are discontinued, while some other new ones are emerging.

The golden thread that seems to be common across all systems and industries is that PM has not delivered primarily because:

1. It is annual
2. It is backward looking
3. It is complex
4. It is time consuming
5. It is inconsistent (CEB 2016)

The Knowledge Resources *HR Survey 2011*, which surveyed 432 organisations employing 1,13 million people, 15 889 of whom were employed in human resource (HR) departments, found that performance management and creating a high-performance culture ranked as the number-one HR priority for the last three years.[1] This handbook will provide you with a practical understanding of what performance management is, how it works, and how it can be used in successfully building a high-performance culture. Most importantly, it will show you that performance management is just as critical as it always was, we just need to use it better – use simpler tools, move towards developmental discussions, and remove or reduce "forced" rankings. Performance management systems have become too time-consuming and cumbersome – the time is right for a reboot.

With the recent headlines and hype around "throw out performance management", many of our clients are asking us – what takes its place, what next? The simple answer is that few are literally throwing performance management (PM) out in its entirety. It is evolving into something more doable and usable.

Performance management is and will always be an integral part of every business. Every manager and business owner without exception, with or without formal training, practises performance management on an intuitive level every day. They may not even know it is called "performance management", but it is permanently on their mind – how to increase the effectiveness of the company by improving the performance of the people who work in it.

Concerns about Performance Management

Performance is obviously an extremely difficult variable to measure, especially in today's rapidly changing organisations. Results and measures become obsolete very quickly, and translating interactions and human desires to measurements may be seen as unlikely and impersonal. This means that a PM system has to be continually evaluated against its goals.

I came across an article by the Boston Consulting Group titled "The Art of Performance Management". I think the authors really got to the gist of why PM systems need to be revamped.[2]

They claim that companies' Chief Financial Officers have increasingly become responsible for the performance aspect of the business, making them the "chief performance officers".

An extract from the article:

> Unfortunately, most CFOs are poorly served in this role by the current state of their company's performance management system. The proliferation of information technology has allowed organizations to generate more data and reports than ever before. The paradoxical result, however, is that senior managers and boards of directors are drowning in a sea of data without the tools needed to translate that data into genuine intelligence and insight about the business.

> At most large companies, the performance management system is a hodgepodge of legacy systems. KPIs are not aligned across the organization. Different information systems categorize data differently – what some parts of the organization define as fixed costs, others define as variable; human resources, finance, and payroll often have different definitions of what constitutes an FTE. Decision rights as to who decides what data to collect are so distributed that there is no consistent approach to reporting across the entire company.

> As a result, the finance organisation spends an inordinate amount of time simply putting the data together and trying to resolve the inconsistencies so that executives can make apples-to-apples comparisons. We estimate that this task consumes roughly 30 percent of the resources in a typical corporate finance function. But the far more serious cost is the negative impact of poor data quality on senior management time and decision making. As one senior executive told us, "Our leadership team spends so much time trying to make sense of the data and debating whether it is right that we never get around to exploring what it really means for the business!"

> CFOs are keenly aware of the problem. "We generate some 20,000 reports every year – one for every three employees! That can't be right", said one. "We've stitched together our performance management system on blood, sweat, and Excel", said another. "It's a controller's nightmare."

Their advice is for companies to stop spending money on new IT systems, to step back and take a more strategic and holistic approach. The company's most important metrics need to be identified in order to help build an organisational system that will translate the data into actionable business insights and more useful decision making.

On a practical level, changes that companies can make to modernise their systems include:

1. Simpler forms
2. Abolishing two rating sessions a year and replacing them with ongoing conversations
3. Removing forced ranking
4. Avoiding moderating performance scores at the expense of line manager authority

This seems to be the trigger for the revolution against PM. It is too time consuming and cumbersome! The initial knee-jerk reaction was – kill it or throw it out. The dust has now settled on a more practical approach – streamlining the process and creating space for a conversation. This book should be read in this context.

1.2. THE GLOBAL, COMPETITIVE MARKETPLACE

How flexible are the HR policies and practices of most companies? The larger the company, the less likely it is to be flexible. Companies that employ thousands of staff cannot afford the time to make exceptions for individuals. Instead, they need to develop processes that cater to the modern-day mantras of cost and process efficiency. Changing operating systems or refining product specifications is relatively easy. The products and systems do not complain. They never embark on go-slows, or initiate industrial action, or burst into floods of tears when told that things need to change. People, on the other hand, tend to require more consideration, more care, and are inevitably more complex.

If highly qualified employees were a dime a dozen, perhaps the level of complexity would remain, but the level of care would diminish. Why bother if staff can easily be replaced? Unfortunately, the demand for talent far exceeds the supply, especially in emerging markets. One of the reasons for this is that companies are growing much faster than the education infrastructure. Another reason is that the available talent pool is much smaller than the raw numbers suggest. Although the numbers of graduates in emerging markets like China and India seem high, research indicates that the quality of their degrees is sometimes not comparable with that of degrees obtained in developed countries. For example, McKinsey believes that only 25 per cent of India's engineering graduates, 15 per cent of its finance and accounting professionals, and 10 per cent of those with degrees of any kind are qualified to work for a multinational company.[3]

This talent pool concern does not only impact emerging economies. Developed economies are also facing competition for talent as emerging economies attract global talent.[4] But it is not only competition for talent, it is making sure that the talent that is available is appropriate, retained, adaptable, agile and able to innovate as the world of work changes – and this means traditional performance management tools may no longer be fit for purpose. Now, more than ever, they need a reboot.

Companies need to find innovative ways to recruit, reward, and retain staff. They also need to find ways of maximising the quality and quantity of their employees' performance in the midst of turbulent economic conditions. Skills gaps need to be bridged and continuous development is essential. In an environment of rapid growth, these challenges become even more demanding.

This handbook serves as a practical and convenient guide to managing performance in an uncertain, turbulent world where companies must adapt. As the world changes, so the management of the performance of the people who drive that change must also adapt. This does not mean the ways in which we have performance-managed people must be thrown out – rather it is how, why and when we use them that is important.

There are a number of methods and tools that can be used for performance management, and every company will need to select the right methods and tools for its environment. There is no one best practice.

Different approaches work for different companies. A good example is China's Haier, a multinational consumer electronics and home appliances company, which has made pay 100 per cent performance-related. It also makes extensive use of "naming and shaming". Photographs of local managers are prominently displayed in every workplace and are marked with a magnetic badge (a red, smiley face for good performance, and a yellow, frowning one for doing badly). The company also celebrates outstanding innovators at public ceremonies, and names new products and business innovations after the people who think them up.[5] This approach would definitely not be welcome in many other companies, but is obviously working well for Haier.

The culture of the company and the territory are important factors when looking at people strategies and performance management. Multinational enterprises in emerging markets are increasingly using cross-cultural, virtual and situational teams to increase speed in launching products to market and in bringing together employees from different locations, functional areas, and cultural perspectives. While the diversity of this type of workforce is a significant source of competitive advantage, the impact of geographic spread and cultural diversity also presents many challenges to conventional management practices. For example, there can be significant differences in how individuals in different cultures provide and seek performance feedback.[6] The definition of what constitutes performance and the consequences of poor performance are also varied.[7]

The Western concept of performance management may not always suit other cultures. The manager–subordinate relationship is often a point of contention owing to power distance or discomfort with critical feedback. For example, in India, it is sometimes seen as inappropriate and disrespectful to disagree with one's supervisor.[8]

One of the purposes of global performance management is to build and maintain a strong, overarching, integrative corporate culture.[9] To achieve this corporate culture, a thorough acknowledgement and understanding of the diversity of local cultures are essential. Training for managers about how to use global performance management systems, including diversity and cultural competency, is vital; otherwise, implementation could well be a waste of time and money.[10] Adequate training must be provided for both the appraiser and the appraisee in order to avoid the many rating errors that are common in performance appraisal. Just because someone is appointed as a manager does not necessarily mean they know how to conduct a performance appraisal or manage performance. Training should include cultural, legal and customer differences by country, thus providing managers with the tools to improve on the process. Managers must also be given the opportunity to build the required relationship with their employees.[11]

Improving performance is a never-ending process, and organisations should strive to achieve the optimum level of cost and profit, as well as gain customer satisfaction and goodwill, and gain potential future business.

1.3. PERFORMANCE MANAGEMENT IN A CHANGING WORLD OF WORK

There are many conceptual models that apply to performance management.[12] From researched works on corporate and leadership longevity[13] to narrations of success (and failure) in works such as *In search of excellence, Built to last, Good to great*,[14] such models abound. As you work through this handbook, you will no doubt discover many of these. When this happens, you should record them and also develop your own overarching conceptual approach to each, particularly as it applies within your organisation.[15]

Without wanting to detract from the various models and approaches available for improving performance, we want to focus your attention fairly practically. In the modern world of business, we are faced with an increasing demand for what is known as "the five horsemen of business change". These are as follows:

- Globality: Global reach – which creates competitors that we never used to have, and internationals competing in our own back yards without the perceived problems that we claim to have.[16]

- Service: Incessant demand for new products and services – which we never needed to have before, and with a much better informed consumer.[17]

- Speed: Technological change at exponential speed – which means that technology is often obsolete as soon as we engage it.[18]

- Quality: Constant, improved-quality demands with increasing thresholds and tolerances – we need to be better and smarter, and we need to make key trade-offs and choices, as we can never be outstanding at everything.[19]

- Value: Lowest possible cost or, alternatively, best possible value for money.[20] We need to drive costs down constantly or give the best perceptual (or real) value.[21]

All this means that we need to be constantly improving and reinventing our performance. The one who stands still has already lost the race!

Global Performance Management Trends in the New World of Work

In 2015 Mercer administered a Global Performance Management Survey including more than 1 050 performance management leaders representing 53 countries.[22] The results show that the changing workplace and world of work are giving rise to new and challenging demands for performance management:

- Employees need to be more agile and autonomous, yet extensive collaboration is required at an unprecedented level.

- Managers, employees and teams are not co-located due to geographic spread, matrix structures and flexible work arrangements.

- Day-to-day work is more project driven.

- Employee engagement levels are increasingly becoming connected to the clear articulation of the relationship between the employees' work and organisational goals.

- Performance management is still perceived as subjective and lack of engagement in the process has gone from bad to worse.

Mercer assert that the key driver of successful performance management is the skill of managers, including how well managers set employee goals, provide feedback, evaluate performance and link performance to critical talent-management decisions. Executive commitment, calibration and technology are also identified as critical drivers of success.

Companies are looking to move performance management from a flight/fear state to a reward state. Changes being considered include:

- calibration in place of moderation
- immediate team and customer feedback to replace annual feedback
- coaching for performance
- an emphasis on peer and manager skills over scoring systems

It is the objective of this textbook to provide you with a set of applicable tools and practices rather than to overburden you with theory.

First, you really need to view the organisation as an adaptive system that relates within and with its environment. Because of both the global and the competitive nature of the modern business world, we must accept that the organisation will be in a dynamic coexistence with its environment.[23] This means that the organisation will both impact on and be impacted on by the environment. When you understand how the organisation actually performs, then you should be able to:

- elaborate on specific frameworks against which you would evaluate an organisation
- decide on appropriate measurement strategies, specifically for organisations
- understand the various issues of organisational performance

1.4. THE THREE LEVELS OF PERFORMANCE MANAGEMENT

Given both the systemic and the adaptive view of organisations, conceptually there are three levels of performance management. All three of these levels should be interrogated to achieve performance improvement.

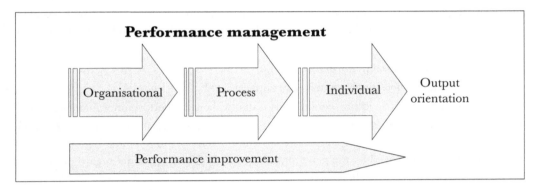

Figure 1.1: The context of performance improvement in an organisational setting
(Source: Huss)

1.4.1. The organisation level

This encompasses the relationship that an organisation has with its markets, and also those major functions that comprise the organisation in its interaction with the external world – the macro-view.

You should consider the following:

- **Organisational goals**, which are the targets towards which the organisation strives. These can well be strategic, such as being number one or two in an industry or sector, or they can be operationally forced on you, for example survival- and turnaround-type goals such as remaining profitable and preventing closure.
- **Organisational design**, which is where the organisational substructure is actually arranged and aligned to match the requirements inherent in achieving the goals. This is the area where HR professionals can make a major contribution.
- **Organisational management**, where the resources are actually performance-managed so that the organisational goals are met. Again, this is an area where HR professionals can play a major role.

You also need to consider the environment and the reality against which the goals are established and met. This comprises the value added by the organisation itself – your organisation's position amongst its competitors and rivals. You may well wish to contextualise your understanding regarding your organisation by investigating the following issues:

- What is your organisation's position in the market, relative to its competitors?

- What are your organisation's goals?
- Has the performance of your organisation improved or deteriorated over time?
- What is performance when applied to your organisation?
- How would you measure organisational performance?
- What drives organisational success in your business?

Once you have an understanding of your own organisation and its key performance variables in the world of work, you should be in a position to answer the following with specific regard to performance criteria:

- Are there any universal performance criteria?
- Are there any models that have universal applicability?
- Is there a performance improvement process that will enable performance management?
- What can we learn from different business sectors and industries about performance within each sector?
- What is the role played by the generally accepted "Western" mind-set regarding business performance? Are there others?
- What is the cultural mind-set of the geography you operate in? There may be many.
- What are the key elements of your own model?

1.4.2. The process level

The process level comprises the internal, micro-view of the systems and procedures that operate within organisations – the value added by the systems within the organisation.

Identify the following:

- What are your organisation's operational best practices?
- Do you have unique "pathfinding" practices and procedures?

Develop a clear understanding of organisational processes by doing the following:

- Identify and focus on the value added by internal processes.
- Determine where possible process problems and bottlenecks occur.
- Understand the various issues of process performance.
- Identify the barriers to process efficiency.

With this understanding in mind, consider the following questions:

- Which new processes should you initiate?
- Which processes should you retain?
- Which processes should you change/improve?

Before you start new processes or consider changing existing processes, you need to ensure that you have the knowledge and skill to investigate and assess processes appropriately.

Changing processes can have both intended and unintended consequences. You need to consider the impact of these consequences from a financial-, HR- and process-efficiency perspective before initiating change.

As part of your knowledge and skills development, make sure you consider these questions:

*   What is the best way to analyse a process?
*   What would you do to implement a lean manufacturing concept?
*   How can you use the value chain in organisational process design?
*   What is the difference between business process re-engineering and organisational development?
*   How best do you empower people within a process-driven environment?
*   How do you measure process improvement?
*   How best do you reward the achievement of strategic deliverables?

As a metaphor, think of a river flowing down from its source through an environment until it eventually flows into the sea and discharges whatever it has carried from the mountains into the sea, together with whatever else it has picked up along the way. The mountain source is the start or initiation, the river the process, and, along the way, what is picked up are steps or sub-assemblies of the eventual product (ie service) – essentially **output** that is discharged into the sea (ie what is sold or delivered to a customer or client).

It is very difficult to go back "upstream" to resolve issues or problems after they have occurred. It is essential to understand the entire process flow, from source to sea (initiation to output) before the process is started. You will need to consider quality and delivery at each stage of the process, and build in quality assessments to pick up problems as they occur. Most importantly, you need to have a clear understanding of what constitutes success so that you can effectively measure the success of your process as well as the quality of the output. If possible, get into a good manufacturing plant and see exactly how various types of processes flow.

1.4.3. The individual level

Recommended reading
In developing a process orientation, it is suggested that you read the work of Eli Goldratt. Eli was the originator of a concept called the Theory of Constraints, and this theory is exceptionally useful in understanding where things can go wrong with processes. The majority of his books are written as business novels and follow a narrative, parable style of writing, with a narrator who takes you through the various issues and principles.

The individual level covers the arena of individual performance, that is, the evaluation of the value added by people within the organisation. The primary purpose of this handbook is to provide a practical understanding of individual performance management. In all cases, we are really concerned with either the role played by people in the specific cluster of performance or, alternatively, the contribution that an HR professional can make to the specific performance issue.

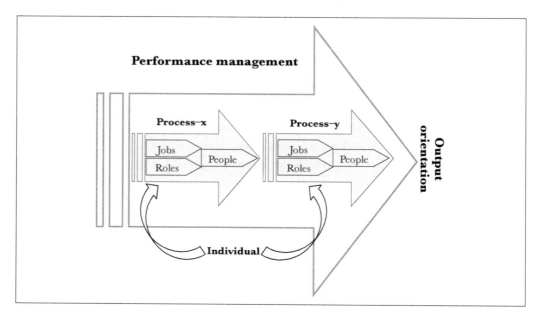

Figure 1.2: Linking individual performance in an organisational context
(Source: Huss)

The performance needs of a company flow directly from the macro-strategy. The ultimate goals of the company determine the "what" and "how" people must perform to achieve these goals. A company will first align the operations, units and functions, and only then align the individual contributors (at the job or role level) to this performance ethic. Practically, this means people need to be aware of how they contribute to the performance needs of the organisation. Having a sense of purpose has been identified as a critical component of employee engagement and serves to promote discretionary effort. An employee's sense of purpose often comes from knowing and understanding the role he or she plays in the performance of the organisation as a whole, and not just within his or her area, unit or process.

This implies that the job or role that the individual performs must be meaningful, first, within the organisational system, and, secondly, in the sense that it must contribute to the eventual success of the organisation. One of the key challenges faced in creating meaning and a sense of purpose for individuals is the fact that organisations and their environments are dynamic and constantly striving toward continuous improvement. In such a fast-paced, changing system, feedback must be given effectively and frequently – there is no time to wait for the annual review. A process of alignment and continuous appraisal is necessary to keep the role and the individual effective within the dynamic environment.

Alignment and appraisal may seem superficially simple, but both are time-consuming, resource-intensive and can become major obstacles to productivity if not properly managed. An example of this is the job description. All employees are entitled to a comprehensive job description that describes the roles and actions they are expected to perform. In a dynamic environment it is difficult to update job descriptions constantly in order to reflect the changing requirements of many positions. As a result, there is often a tendency for the "work-to-rule" approach to be present, where employees only do what is laid down in the job description, invoking a particular attitude around issues of entitlement and contract.

In reality:

- Jobs are dynamic and rarely static.
- Job descriptions are out of date even before they are published.
- Job descriptions should be viewed as guidelines rather than recipes.
- The input–output boundary is still prevalent in many managers' minds – their history makes them focus on inputs and activities rather than required outputs and performance.

1.5. CONCLUSION

Performance management thus requires an understanding of the environment, the organisation, the processes within the organisation, and the contribution of individuals to the organisation. Although this handbook focuses on the individual component of performance management, it is essential that you bear the wider components of performance management in mind at all times. Individuals do not work in a vacuum and cannot be managed in isolation from their environmental and organisational ecologies.

The following are the questions and issues that you should focus on for this theme:

- How best can you cascade the overall performance goals of the organisation into individual performance criteria at the job/role level?
- What is the key contribution that people as individuals make to the organisation?
- What should a motivating working environment look like?
- How would you create outstanding performers at all levels of the organisation?
- What role should emotional balance, that is, the aspirations and goals of individuals, play in output-orientated performance criteria?
- How would you hold a performance conversation? How often?
- What strategies would you implement for nonperformers?
- What is the role of the manager in the individual performance arena?
- What is the role of HR in the individual performance arena?
- What is the role of the individual in the individual performance arena?
- What is an individual development plan?
- How would you draw up an individual balanced scorecard?
- What would it look like?

1.6. BIBLIOGRAPHY

Ackerman, R. 2001. *Hearing grasshoppers jump*. Cape Town: David Philip.

Ackerman, R. 2005. *The four legs of the table*. Cape Town: David Philip.

Albrecht, K. 1993. *The only thing that matters*. New York: Harper Business.

Appelbaum, SH, Roy, M & Gilliland, T. 2011. Globalization of performance appraisals: theory and applications. *Management Decision* 49(4):570-585.

Armstrong, M & Baron, A. 2003. *Performance management*. London: Chartered Institute for Personnel and Development.

Ball, A & Asbury, S. 1989. *The winning way*. Johannesburg: Jonathan Ball.

Bass, BM. 1985. *Leadership and performance beyond expectations*. New York: The Free Press.

Bower, M. 1997. *The will to lead*. Boston: Harvard Business School Press.

Boyett, JH & Conn, HP. 1995. *Maximum performance management*. Oxford: Capstone.

Carlzon, J. 1987. *Moments of truth*. New York: Harper Collins.

Cascio, WF. 2006. Global performance management system, in *Handbook of research in international human resource management*, edited by GK Stahl & I Björkman. Cheltenham: Edward Elgar.

Chartered Management Institute. 2003. *Six weeks to professional excellence*. London: Hodder & Stoughton.

Collins, JC. 2001. *Good to great*. London: Random House.

Collins, JC & Porras, JI. 2000. *Built to last*. London: Random House.

Corporate Research Foundation. 2000. *The best companies to work for in South Africa*. Cape Town: Zebra.

Corporate Research Foundation. 2001. *Top ICT companies in South Africa*. Cape Town: Zebra.

Crainer, S. 1999. *The 75 greatest management decisions ever made*. New York: Amacom.

De Geus, A. 1997. *The living company*. Boston: Harvard Business School Press.

Dell, M. 1999. *Direct from Dell*. London: Harper Collins Business.

Economist (The). 15 April 2010. *Grow, grow, grow. What makes emerging-market companies run*. Retrieved from: http://www.economist.com/node/15879405/print on 31 January 2012.

Evans, P, Pucik, V & Barsoux, JL. 2002. *The global challenge: frameworks for international human resource management*. Boston: McGraw-Hill.

Faull, N. 1998. *Competitive capabilities*. Cape Town: Juta.

Furlonger, D. 2004. 50 top companies to work for, *Financial Mail* 178.

Heller, R. 1997. *In search of European excellence*. London: Harper Collins.

Hellqvist, N. 2011. Global performance management: a research agenda. *Management Research Review* 34(8):927-946.

Knowledge Resources. 2011. *HR Survey 2011*. South Africa.

Kotzen, J., Nolan, T., Plaschke, F., Tucker, J., & Ghesquieres, J. March 2015. *The Art of Performance Management*. The Boston Consulting Group. Retrieved from: http://www.wiwi.uni-passau.de/fileadmin/dokumente/lehrstuehle/obermaier/Lehre/Gastvortr%C3%A4ge_und_Exkursionen/The_Art_of_Performance_Management_Mar_2015.pdf on 14 March 2017.

Lombardi, Jr, V. 2002. *What it takes to be #1*. New York: McGraw-Hill.

Mail & Guardian. 2000. *Movers and shakers: the A-Z of South African business people*. London: Penguin.

Mercer. 2015. *Global Performance Management Survey*. Retrieved from: https://www.imercer.com/products/2013/performance.aspx on 26 February 2017.

Mercer. 2016. *Future proofing HR*. Retrieved from: https://www.mercer.com/content/dam/mercer/attachments/private/nurture-cycle/global-talent-hr-trends-report-2016-mercer.pdf on 15 February 2017.

Milliman, J, Taylor, S & Czaplewski, AJ. 2002. Cross-cultural performance feedback in multinational enterprises: opportunity for organisational learning. *Human Resource Planning* 25.

Moore-Ede, A. 1993. *The twenty four hour society*. Reading, Massachusetts: Addison-Wesley.

Neff, TJ & Citrin, JM. 2000. *Lessons from the top*. London: Penguin.

Nightingale Multimedia. 1999. *The 100 best companies to work for in the UK*. London: Hodder & Stoughton Educational.

Peters, TJ & Waterman, RH. 1982. *In search of excellence*. New York: Harper Row.

Rummler, GA & Brache, AP. 1995. *Improving performance*. San Francisco: Jossey-Bass.

Ulrich, D. 1999. *Results-based leadership*. Boston: Harvard Business School Press.

Warwick Manufacturing Group. (n.d.). *Time compression self-help guide*. Coventry: Warwick Manufacturing Group.

Womack, JP & Jones, DT. 1996. *Lean thinking*. London: Simon & Schuster.

Endnotes

1. Knowledge Resources, 2011.
2. Kotzen, Nolan, Plaschke, Tucker, & Ghesquieres, 2015.
3. *The Economist*, 2010.
4. Mercer, 2016.
5. *The Economist*, 2010.
6. Milliman, Taylor & Czaplewski, 2002.
7. Evans, Pucik & Barsoux, 2002.
8. Evans, Pucik & Barsoux, 2002; Cascio, 2006.
9. Hellqvist, 2011.
10. Cascio, 2006.
11. Appelbaum, Roy & Gilliland, 2011.
12. Armstrong & Baron, 2003; Bass, 1985; Boyett & Conn, 1995; Rummler & Brache, 1995; Ulrich, 1999.
13. De Geus, 1997.
14. Peters & Waterman, 1982; Collins & Porras, 2000; Collins, 2001.
15. Ackerman, 2005; Faull, 1998.
16. Ackerman, 2001; Lombardi, 2002.
17. Albrecht, 1993; Carlzon, 1987; Moore-Ede, 1993.
18. Crainer, 1999; Womack & Jones, 1996; Warwick Manufacturing Group, (n.d).
19. Chartered Management Institute 2003.
20. Dell, 1999.
21. Bower, 1997; Furlonger, 2004; Nightingale Multimedia, 1999; Neff & Citrin, 2000.
22. Mercer, 2015.
23. Ball & Asbury, 1989; Heller, 1997; Corporate Research Foundation, 2000; Corporate Research Foundation, 2001; *Mail & Guardian*, 2000.

2 THE PHILOSOPHY OF PERFORMANCE

2.1. INTRODUCTION

Many people are threatened by both the process and surrounding activity of performance management. This is mainly because managers use the process to wield "the big stick" of punishment in a negative rather than a positive way. The reality is that, with sound use, performance management can actually become a positive, daily conversation that leads to better results and performance throughout the organisation. The key to this is the understanding that the overall philosophy of performance management is development – improved people performance leads to improved company performance.

The performance management process is a cascade of the strategic and operational requirements of the organisation down to an individual level. Each individual needs to understand fully and exactly what and where he or she contributes to the final result in the total picture for the organisation.

To understand individual contributions to the organisation, it is important to:

*   understand Business. Here, we mean the overarching, external business model within the total market or economy whereby you manufacture products, provide services and then provide these for a client base, thereby making a business profit – or adding some form of value. Essentially, how do you either make money (profit) or, alternatively, add value (often more of an issue in public or service organisations)?
*   understand "the business". Here, you really need to get to grips with the specific business that you are operating in. Far too often, human resource (HR) practitioners are criticised for being too discipline- or function-focused, being too "airy-fairy", not having their feet firmly on the ground, and being too theoretical. This really means that, whatever business you are in, you must actually understand how it operates. We really cannot stress the importance of this "hands-on" practical knowledge enough.
*   understand your specific discipline or function. In our view, only once you have a good handle on the previous two arenas, can you make a difference with your area of specialty, whatever that is. This is where the tools and techniques of your chosen profession become important and inform part of your ability to perform.

Once you have grasped the concept of performance and have understood the realities and contexts of the business you are in, you are ready to tackle the process of individual performance management.

2.2. WHAT IS PERFORMANCE MANAGEMENT?

Despite its critical importance, a study conducted by the University of Stellenbosch Business School[24] revealed that the organisations studied displayed a negative culture regarding performance management, that corporate strategic focus areas were not aligned with the performance areas of individuals lower down in the organisation, and that there was generally a lack of support for performance management by line managers.

If research has proven that performance management positively influences sales, reduces absenteeism, and increases productivity and safety,[25] the question that needs to be asked is: Why are so many organisations still grappling with the sound implementation of performance management? Also, why are performance appraisals generally feared by employees and why do supervisors experience such appraisals as a stressful process? If we know that performance management is so essential, why do people approach it with such resignation and resistance? It is important that the philosophy of performance permeates management across all levels of the organisation.

Let's start by covering some basic principles.

Performance management is a process that measures individual employee performance against set performance standards. The objectives of performance management are defined as follows:
- to align organisational and individual goals
- to foster organisation-wide commitment to a performance-oriented culture
- to develop and manage the human resources needed to achieve organisational results
- to identify and address performance inefficiencies
- to create a culture of accountability and a focus on customer service
- to link rewards to performance[26]

2.3. THE PERFORMANCE MANAGEMENT PROCESS

The real issue in performance management is to ensure that the organisation meets its overall objectives. This requires an integrated approach whereby the individual on the front line (or coalface) actually understands exactly what his or her role is in the intended outputs of the organisation. With this understanding, he or she can be held accountable for individual performance parameters according to a specific design. There are various ways in which this design can be achieved, but it all begins with a look at the overall strategy of the organisation. Sound leadership within the organisation ensures that there is a determined vision which the organisation will follow, that this is turned into a set of goals and objectives, and that the various resources are aligned to match or meet the specific objectives. This, in itself, is a process that can usually be depicted cyclically. The WorldatWork approach sets out the following process:

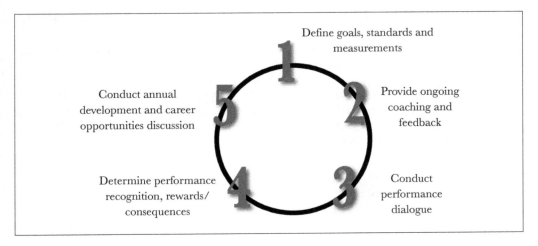

Figure 2.1: Performance management process phases[27]

The performance management process is designed to involve both managers and reports in each part of the cycle. The cycle can take place quarterly, semi-annually or annually. The most common approach is twice a year. Notice that the process is a circle; it is an unbroken cycle of communication between the manager and employee.

The phases of the performance management process are as follows:

Phase 1:   Define goals, standards and measurements
Phase 2:   Provide ongoing coaching and feedback
Phase 3:   Conduct performance dialogue
Phase 4:   Determine performance recognition, rewards or consequences
Phase 5:   Conduct annual development and career opportunities discussion

Typically, phases 1 through 4 cover the actual process that is usually addressed within the total rewards spectrum of an organisation. One of the most important aspects of the performance management process is actually phase 5 – the individual development and career opportunity offered by the process. Far too often, the cycle is linked to a reward-management process rather than a development process, and so necessary synergies are lost. Oftentimes employees will "tune out" of the performance discussion, waiting for the rating and what that means for their remuneration, bonus or position.

Much of the recent literature actually stresses introducing the above phases at different times, but also emphasises coaching and feedback. Practically, this would mean that phase 2 on coaching and feedback is given a lot more prominence, even within the performance discussion. To ensure consistent improvement and development, the feedback – both positive and negative – must be as close to the event or behaviour as possible, and must be constructive.

The performance dialogue can then focus on the performance that is linked to ultimate achievement of the goals. And since the continuous feedback has been happening throughout the performance period, there should be no surprises for the manager or employee.

It is also recommended that the performance discussion happens at a different time to the discussion about remuneration – even a month apart. If the two are done together, employees often stop listening to the review and focus on the money discussion, and the process loses some of its effectiveness, leading to frustration.[28]

An important consideration for this handbook is the customer focus of the approach. It is not enough to understand just the strategic importance of the role. It is also critical that the specific customer focus and customer orientation are established. The following figure (Figure 2.2) gives an indication of customer relativity within this process.

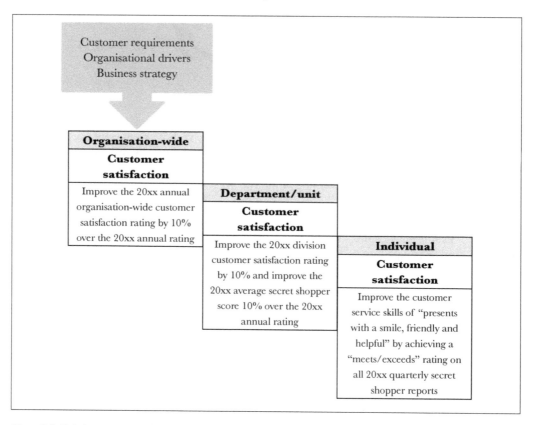

Figure 2.2: Relative customer goal alignment at the various organisational levels

Customer requirements, organisational drivers and business strategy lead to the development of specific organisational performance objectives. These objectives include a variety of clearly identified, measurable goals that need to be attained to achieve the business strategy.

2.3.1. Phase 1: Define goals, standards and measures

Goal alignment – performance must be aligned with the strategic goals of the organisation. The first step in developing an effective performance management system is determining the organisation's objectives, and then translating these into departmental and, ultimately, individual goals.[29] Goals should evolve from the mission and vision of the organisation, and should be communicated downward. In this way, everyone knows what the objectives of the organisation are, and everyone is involved in the achievement of the organisational goals. The linking of individual employee goals to the organisational goals therefore contributes to the achievement of results.[30] Objectives or goals define what organisations, functions, departments, teams and individuals are expected to achieve.[31]

In addition to setting individual goals, employees must state the various plans they will use to achieve these goals, and how the goals will be measured. Each individual's goals should align with his or her manager's goals, thereby giving a clear line of sight to the organisation-wide goals and business strategy. This point cannot be emphasised enough – the CIPD compares goals to prescribed medicine – it works, but only if it is the right medicine, given at the right dosage. Goals must be the right ones, aligned properly, and at a level that is achievable but with some challenge.[32]

Performance management then takes place by way of a conversation or dialogue between the individual employee and his or her manager where goals are aligned and their achievability and evaluation are addressed.

It is not enough that the specific goals be set. These goals also need to be linked to specific desired outputs which become the requisite performance standards (expected outcomes). The trick is to identify the most meaningful drivers for your own organisation or context. This is often linked to the type and complexity of the job. A target of "produce 5 widgets per day" is a clear output that aligns to a role that is well defined. This does not work for senior managers in complex organisations. These goals should link to an outcome, such as "build an effective change management team".

Simply put, for all goals, the way to develop them is to:

- select a strategic perspective (actually formulated as a strategic objective)
- examine how best to implement this strategy
- find two or three measurable drivers that would immediately signal that you are making progress or have achieved your strategic goal. (These drivers then become the **strategic performance drivers.**)

(Olve, Jan & Wetter, 2000)

With input from the employee, performance standards should be developed for each job. Here is an example of a performance standard:

> Job duty: Deliver mail to each department daily – performance standard: Deliver the mail with **100% accuracy** to each department by **10:00** daily.

The four most common types of performance standards include the following:

1. **Quality** – how well a duty or activity is performed
2. **Quantity** – how much, or the volume of work, an employee performs
3. **Time** – when a duty is to be performed
4. **Process** – steps or procedures necessary to complete a job duty

Although developing performance standards requires time and resources, it produces an objective and legally defensible appraisal.

Once the criteria of assessment have been established, we are in a position to apply specific performance measures. These can be the following:

1. **Direct observation** – the leader directly observes the employee's performance.

2. **Documented examples** – someone provides documented examples of the employee's performance, such as a project leader documenting a team member's performance on a project, or customer complaints and compliments.

3. **Data-based** – the most objective method; it involves quantified data that can be measured and tracked.

In the record-keeping process that follows, judgement is applied to the method of rating whereby the information obtained from the measurement criteria is used to rate each standard individually. Typically, a structured approach is used where levels of rating are applied to the data assimilated. Depending on the organisation, there may be up to 10 ratings.

Once this writing process is complete, the mechanics of the performance management process can begin. In essence, the work is just beginning as we move into the developmental phases of the performance management system.

2.3.2. Phase 2: provide ongoing coaching and feedback

Throughout the performance management process, managers and their reports should continue to discuss progress. By far the best approach is that of an ongoing performance conversation. In some businesses, strategies and objectives change quickly, sometimes every few months. In such cases, managers and employees may need to change their goals to match those of the changed business objectives.

One of the most important parts of the performance management approach is the need to note the various changes in perspective or direction. Far too often, a performance conversation is held when objectives have not been met, but the underlying criteria have actually changed and not been noted. It is extremely important that all changes to the original parameters are noted so that the actual performance is fairly assessed. The performance conversation can easily become a witch-hunt where employees are blamed for not meeting goals, rather than a proactive discussion of true performance.

Two-way communication is at the heart of the performance management process. To encourage two-way communication, it is important for both the manager and the employee to check in frequently throughout the performance cycle to talk about progression toward goals. In successful performance management systems, employees seek this conversation regularly. The role of the manager then becomes that of coach – conversations are ongoing, face-to-face, open, honest, and provide positive and timeous information for those carrying out the work, so that they can monitor their own performance and enhance the probability of success. (Please remember that the coaching conversation is really one whereby the manager guides the employee and enables him or her to perform. It is important that the manager does not get frustrated and take over the actual performance, usually just because he or she can.)

Notwithstanding the coaching role, it is also important that a form of oversight or monitoring be established. In better performance management situations, employees are responsible for monitoring their own performance and for asking for help as needed (empowerment rather than domination). This promotes employee ownership of, and control over, the process. As employees assess the behavioural changes they need to make, they ask for their manager's feedback. This essentially compares performance against goals to evaluate progress and can be beneficial in helping employees to improve their performance. Managers can assist employees in re-evaluating their direction and re-prioritising their efforts.

The CIPD[33] points out that coaching and feedback sessions are more effective if they are frequent, timely, and focus on shaping successful behaviours and strategies rather than over-analysing weaknesses. It works better to analyse what went well in order to repeat it – the feedforward method. CIPD describe a study by Budworth[34] where some managers were trained in this feedforward method, while the others received other training. These managers' direct reports then got their performance feedback. Four months later, the employees in the feedforward group received higher ratings by independent observers.

Recently, Deloitte moved towards a future-view rather than rating past performance[35] joining the likes of Adobe and Accenture. In a survey of their managers, Deloitte found that more than half were not happy with the old way of managing performance, and a survey of staff found that staff wanted to be coached, developed and guided to become better experts in their fields of work – a vision that aligned with the organisation's vision to be a leading intelligence company. Changes they introduced included employee as well as manager performance reviews, more frequent development sessions, and a focus on discussion rather than rating. The intention was to move from performance management as a means for remuneration towards performance coaching as a means for development.

Some other tips from CIPD[36] on more effective – and more fairly perceived – feedback include:

- Focus on strengths and analyse how they can be used again.
- Listen actively – this means letting the employee mention incidents they view positively, listening to their views and asking questions.
- Conversation is more two-way, rather than the manager listing events and issuing directions.

Feedback – more often, more relevant, more specific

Microsoft, Accenture, Adobe, Gap, Medtronic and Deloitte are revitalizing and reviewing their performance management systems to be less cumbersome, time consuming and "old-fashioned". These companies believe that the traditional approach to performance management and review is no longer suitable. As seen in Chapter 1, the world of work has changed, and so too, they contend, should the measurement of the people who work there. It is not only the measurement process that needs to be adapted, but also the quantity and nature of the feedback provided to employees.

Feedback – more often, more relevant, more specific (continued)

Giving feedback only once or twice a year is not helpful in a fast-paced, immediate impact workplace. In many ways, the actual rating or ranking process (if it is used at all) is less important than what is provided as feedback to employees. Marr[37] offers the following suggestions:

- **Make feedback about the person** – focus the feedback on the person in their own role, not as compared to others, possibly in other departments or even countries. Rather focus on the role and performance against the role.

- **Give feedback more often** – feedback provided close to the time of the activity is much more effective than that provided once or twice a year. Feedback should be both positive and negative and can be given at any time, in any place. It does not always have to be in a formal meeting room. One tip for managers is keep documentation of the feedback, even when it is informal.

- **Focus on the future** – feedback can draw on what has happened in the immediate past as a basis but really should focus on how to do the same thing again in future, or change it for the future. This is a *strengths based approach* – it focuses on how the employee can continue the behaviour, enhance it, or change something that didn't work. This constant, gradual "course correction" is much more effective than trying to "turn the whole ship 180 degrees" at once.

Marr[38] makes the point that the abovementioned changes in the nature, frequency and style of feedback lead to better employee performance. The move is from "dwelling on the past" towards "moving to the future". A subtle but important shift in motivating and enhancing performance.

2.3.3. Phase 3: conduct performance appraisal and evaluation discussion (the formal process)

As a supplement to the ongoing communication process and to minimise the chance of surprises for the manager or the employee, it is important to hold periodic discussions or reviews. Some businesses require quarterly dialogues, while others require semi-annual or annual reviews. More often than not, these are aligned to reward and pay processes rather than real performance management. In essence, during the year-end review, the dialogue centres on the employee's accomplishments and shortfalls for the year.

There are several widely used methods of conducting performance appraisals with employees. By far the most common method uses the goal-setting or management by objectives (MBO) method. In this approach, clear and precisely defined goal statements for the work to be done by an employee are established. These goals must be quantifiable and measurable before being included in an MBO plan. The manager and employee establish a plan indicating how these goals are to be achieved. The manager ensures that the employee has the required resources, training and competence to complete the goals specified. An agreed period of time is allowed during which the employee is given an opportunity to implement the plan, and then goal achievement is measured. At specific nodal points, corrective action can be taken and new goals or amendments can be added to the original plan. All of these require the active participation of the employee in the goal-setting process.

In conducting the actual appraisal conversation, the manager/appraiser needs to do the following:

- Allow enough time – schedule in advance and allow sufficient time for the meeting.
- Maintain confidentiality – the appraiser should not share results with other employees. In addition, a location which protects the confidentiality of the meeting should be chosen.
- Review input – in preparation for the meeting, the appraiser should ask the employee for his or her accomplishments during the period being evaluated.
- Clarify performance issues – the appraiser should provide specific information about performance deficiencies.
- Be specific about the performance rating – help the employee develop and grow in his or her work by giving a truthful rating, even if it is not positive.
- Offer assistance – offer an improvement plan to help the employee.
- Provide ongoing feedback about performance – remember to give feedback often, not just during an annual evaluation.

2.3.4. Phase 4: determine performance rewards/consequences

In this important phase, the relationship between the performance management system and the reward system is clearly established. Sometime after the performance review has taken place, the manager should utilise the salary-planning guidelines to determine the appropriate reward and/or consequence which compares actual performance with agreed goals and outputs. Performance rewards are given through merit pay or extra payment such as a cash bonus.

Fundamentally, there are two main sets of criteria which need to be established:

- the achievement of the goal itself – whether or not the goal was achieved
- the extent or standard of performance with which the goal was achieved

This means that the way the employee met the defined standards of quality, quantity, time and process will determine, to a great extent, the reward or consequence.

2.3.5. Phase 5: the annual development and career opportunities evaluation and discussion

Far too few organisations actually incorporate their overall succession planning and talent management as part of an ongoing performance management system. What is really required is that each employee understands exactly where he or she fits in terms of talent management. This means that some way needs to be found whereby individual aspirations and organisational needs, in terms of talent, are matched. Good systems will allow individuals to have input into their career paths within the organisation. Very good systems will even modify and adapt job or role descriptors to suit the specific talents of the individuals. More often than not, organisations are paternalistic and have set ideas regarding job outputs and the requirements of specific roles in the organisation. Innovative organisations will rather maximise the talents of individuals than have hard-and-fast rules regarding the positions they fill.

Key questions for consideration:

- What are some of the performance standards used in your organisation?
- What kinds of measurement criteria are used in your organisation?
- How do managers in your company coach or mentor their reports?
- How often are performance appraisals done in your organisation?
- Can you give some best practices for conducting performance appraisals?
- How best can you maximise the use of the talent resources within your organisation?
- Are some positions or role descriptions constraining and impeding progress or performance?

There are a number of challenges that are commonly encountered in performance management systems. These challenges can lead to performance management being used for purposes for which it was not designed; and also to the dilution of the power of performance management as a tool for development. Some of these challenges include the following:

- Organisations with the process vested in management believe that the appraisal process is actually the appraisal form.
- Appraisal sessions are held too close to one another and are therefore inexorably tied to the increment given.
- Many processes advocate multiple ratings per year, but, owing to many issues, these are not conducted.
- The appraisal process is often one-sided, with a top-down assessment and then a required sign-off by the incumbent.
- Appraisals are seldom dynamic objectives. They are set at the start of the period and are never adjusted, in spite of dynamic movements within the business.
- Appraisals incorporate activities and inputs rather than outputs.
- Management's memories of foul-ups transcend the good times.
- Efforts to make the process objective result in systems including some form of quantitative metrics, with little or no regard for qualitative aspects.
- Metrics are often summarised and overall average ratings given with little or no regard for pockets of excellence.
- Modern appraisals advocate 360-degree approaches, and these are often fraught with internal politics.
- Managers are reluctant to give poor appraisals as they want to be seen to be "the good guys" which results in a skewed distribution by default.
- Managers are reluctant to deal with the consequences of poor individual performance.
- Managers do not know how to stretch the good performers.
- Many appraisal sessions focus on the individual's personality and style rather than actual, concrete performance criteria and evidence.
- Many appraisals are comparative and competitive, where the individual is compared with somebody else and not against his or her own objectives.
- Appraisal sessions are often dreaded by both parties rather than being looked forward to.

To avoid some of these challenges, you should consider the following:

- **Self-appraisal systems** – when output criteria are well established and the actual measurements are really in the hands of the incumbent (as with an appropriate balanced scorecard), there is no reason why the individual cannot do his or her own appraisal. This has the added advantage of allowing the manager to be facilitative and helpful rather than judgemental.

- Think about frequency and have **daily performance conversations** – initially, this could take a long time, but, as the skill develops, the conversation works by exception and, again, is facilitative and helpful rather than defensive and defeatist.

- Develop the habit of "**notes for the record**" that document all project changes and agreed performance amendments – memories are short.

- Allow for at least six formal sessions of **review** for the record for each cycle.

- Seek **appraisal yourself**, learn to use the feedback constructively, adapt, readjust, and then seek another appraisal soon; show your willingness to learn.

- Make **appraisals developmental sessions** rather than acrimonious, pay-related activities.

Above all, look for innovative ways of performing above the expectations you have of yourself – achieving this reward is often far greater than any other.

People are not all the same – what role does personality play?

While the research shows that a strengths-based, developmental performance management process achieves better results, what happens if this does not fit in with the personality of the manager? Over and above this, how does the employee's personality affect the process?

Not everyone is good at noticing or managing various personalities, but becoming aware of the impact of the performance and feedback process on other people is essential. Taking the time to get to know your team is a critical component of being a good manager. It is a well-known fact that the relationship between a manager and employee has the potential to make or break the employee experience. Employees do not want managers who blindly follow a process, especially when it is related to something as important as career progression and pay. Just as it is good practice to get to know your employees' personal preferences when it comes to leadership/management style, it is equally important to tailor performance feedback in a way that suits their personalities. Some employees may thrive on informal feedback while others may prefer to schedule time specifically to discuss performance.

Having an awareness of levels of self-efficacy, understanding what motivates employees, and empowering your team members in ways that best suit their personalities will go a long way to making sure feedback lands well. Processes provide structure and governance, but employees are still individuals and will require a personal approach.

CIPD[39] add a step to the appraisal process – check in on the employee after the appraisal. Appraisals and discussions about performance are more effective when the employee feels they are fair, and that they are empowered to make the changes necessary to do better. During and after the session, ask employees about their feelings and reactions to the appraisal – fair sessions lead to improvement while punitive sessions are just demotivating.

Who are we missing? The Gig Economy

Younger and Smallwood highlight an important but missing group from the performance management system – the percentage of the workforce that is outsourced, including freelancers, consultants, gigsters. This "agile" talent is often neglected or just omitted from the performance review process despite the fact that they are making up more and more of the workforce. Businesses need to ensure this group is included in the performance review process of the company. They suggest the following factors that should be considered for agile talent:[40]

- Share context – make sure all employees are included in critical discussions.
- Measurement should be more than just output, deadlines met and quality, but should also link to softer issues like "cultural fit".
- Sessions for quick, immediate feedback should be provided.
- Make sure the managers assigned to agile talent are the right ones, with a clear emphasis on development.
- Show recognition when it is deserved.

It can be tempting to think of agile talent as a non-permanent workforce that is not worth the same time and effort as full-time employees. This short-term approach may save time initially, but as the new world of work demands more feature and project teams that can be deployed as and when required, having a cohort of outsourced talent who know, understand and buy-in to your business can be invaluable. It is also important to acknowledge that while working in your company, agile talent interacts with full-time members of staff and can have either a positive or negative impact on the employee experience depending on whether they feel part of the team. Spend the time developing agile talent, include them in performance management, give them regular feedback ... pay it forward. The returns you reap will far outweigh the costs.

2.4. CONCLUSION

The key challenge in performance management is to ensure that the outcome of the process is one that benefits the organisation and the employee. The organisation seeks to maximise performance, while the employee seeks valid and constructive feedback to foster development and success in the workplace. These should not be seen as trade-offs. Performance management is an opportunity to communicate to employees their personal role in the success of the organisation and to evaluate their outputs against agreed performance standards. The prospective success of the process is heavily dependent on the underlying philosophy of performance management which the organisation chooses to adopt.

The following are the questions and issues that you should focus on for this theme:

- How would you distinguish between jobs and role profiles?
- What method would you use to ensure that your role profiles are output-oriented?
- How would you ensure that any conflicts between organisational performance objectives and individual wants and desires are resolved and even incorporated into an appropriate role profile? Is this desirable? Why/why not?
- How would you design an effective appraisal process?
- How best can you ensure that the measures used are within the control of the incumbent being appraised?
- How would you align individual objectives with organisational strategies and performance?
- Describe the key elements of an appraisal conversation.
- What would you do to ensure that job criteria and not personality or behavioural style criteria are measured?
- What is the key role of the supervisor? And his or her own superior's role?
- What would you do to ensure that a performance conversation leads to lasting change and/or individual development?
- What would your role description look like?
- What would your appraisal form look like?
- What is the role of HR in this process?

2.5. BIBLIOGRAPHY

Amaratunga, D & Baldry, D. 2002. Moving from performance measurement to performance management. *Facilities* 20(5-6), 217-223.

Armstrong, M. 1996. *A handbook of personnel management practice*. London: Kogan.

Bateman, TS & Snell, SA. 2009. *Management: Leading & collaborating in the competitive world*. 8th edition. New York: McGraw-Hill.

Boice, DF & Kleiner, BH. 1997. Designing effective performance appraisal systems. *Work Study Journal* 46(6) 197-201. USA: California State University.

Buckingham, M & Goodall, A. (2015). Reinventing performance management. *Harvard Business Review*, April, 2015.

CIPD. 2016. *Could do better? Assessing what works in performance management*. Retrieved from: https://www.cipd.co.uk/knowledge/fundamentals/people/performance/what-works-in-performance-management-report on 15 February 2017.

Deloitte (n.d.). Retrieved from http://blog.impraise.com/360-feedback/deloitte-joins-adobe-and-accenture-in-dumping-performance-reviews-360-feedback on 10 February 2017.

Fisher, M. 1998. *Performance appraisals*. The Sunday Times business skills. London: Kogan.

Grobler, P, Wärnich, S, Carrell, MR, Elbert, NF & Hatfield, RD. 2006. *Human resource management in South Africa*. 3rd edition. Thomson Learning.

Kaplan, RS & Norton, DP. 2001. *The strategy focused organisation*. Boston: Harvard Business School.

Marr, R. 2015. *How Accenture and Deloitte Got Rid of Performance Reviews – And You Can Too*. Retrieved from https://www.linkedin.com/pulse/how-accenture-deloitte-got-rid-performance-reviews-you-bernard-marr on 22 February 2017.

Olve, N-Gn, Jan, R & Wetter, M. 2000. *Performance drivers*. West Sussex, England: John Wiley & Sons.

WorldatWork. 2007. *Total rewards management.* Scottsdale, Arizona.

Younger, J. & Smallwood, N. 2016. Performance management in the gig economy. *Harvard Business Review* January 11, 2016.

Endnotes

24. Grobler et al., 2006.
25. Grobler et al., 2006.
26. Armstrong, 1996.
27. WorldatWork, 2007.
28. CIPD, 2016.
29. Boice & Kleiner, 1997.
30. Bateman & Snell, 2009.
31. Fisher, 1998.
32. CIPD, 2016.
33. CIPD, 2016.
34. Budworth et al., 2015.
35. Buckingham & Goodall, 2015.
36. CIPD, 2016.
37. Marr, 2015.
38. Marr, 2015.
39. CIPD, 2016.
40. Younger and Smallwood, 2016.

3 MEASUREMENT AND METRICS

3.1. INTRODUCTION

The term "measurement" is tied to several aspects of performance management. The act of measuring is an analytical skill that is of substantial and even critical importance in modern organisations or industries. In addition, the results of measures can be utilised as tools in guiding an organisational entity through many obstacles and changing requirements posed by customers and the competition. As such, measurement is the primary tool for communicating direction, establishing accountability, defining roles, allocating resources, monitoring and evaluating performance, designing and allocating development programmes, linking organisational process and performance goals, and for implementing changes.[41]

AXIOMS OF PERFORMANCE MEASUREMENT

"What you see is what you measure"

"What you measure is what you get"

"What gets measured, gets managed"

and its converse

"What doesn't get measured, gets forgotten"

Figure 3.1: Axioms of measurement (Cook nd)

3.2. WHY MEASURE?

Measurement is not a "one size fits all" process

Performance management is intricately tied to measurement, but:

- how can we evaluate someone's performance without standardised hard measurements?
- how do we assign a performance bonus or salary increase if we cannot compare performers?
- without the formal measurement of performance, will we be able to make a case if a legal process needs to be followed?

Sound familiar? The most common mistake people make is not in omitting to measure performance or implementing structured processes, but rather in not designing performance

---

Measurement is not a "one size fits all" process (continued)

Measures that best meet their objectives and outcomes. If you need an assembly line performance managed, then quantity measures and quality measures will be important – *x widgets, produced to y specification in one month*. But this process won't work for senior managers running a multinational company.

This chapter sets out what factors to consider in designing and implementing your performance measures – what will suit the culture of the organisation, what will suit the tasks at hand and what best suits the outcomes needed. There are numerous intended and unintended consequences attached to what you measure and how you measure it.

You may be attracting and rewarding the very people you don't want to hire with your performance management system. For example, the type of people who respond well to forced rankings, comparing themselves to others at all costs, tend to be those who are able to "play the game". These employees make sure they are particularly impressive during performance review time and often compete with team members to get a bigger score instead of delivering on overall project objectives. If individual performance is valued more highly than team objectives and outcomes, this kind of behaviour is encouraged and can lead to project failure, even when there are multiple "shining stars" in the team.[42]

Performance management in general is tightly tied to measurement. Measurement allows for the evaluation of changes in performance and provides opportunities to reward appropriate performance (both in terms of salary policy and organisational or developmental opportunities). Furthermore, measurement can aid the process of identifying alternatives on how to solve problems and identify new units of rewards – not necessarily financial.

Measurements of performance give managers a yardstick for packing and managing performance. Some of the benefits are the following:

- Communicating performance expectations to subordinates in the organisation.
- A tangible basis for knowing what is going on in the organisation.
- Assisting with the identification of performance gaps that should be analysed and eliminated.
- Providing feedback to compare performance of employees with a standard and allowing certain behaviours to be rewarded.
- Facilitating key decision making regarding resources, plans, policies, schedules and structure.
- From an employee perspective, measures form the basis for employees to know what is expected of their performance and allow them to monitor their own performance and generate their own feedback. Furthermore, the employees can identify their own gaps or shortcomings in performance and improve upon them.
- From a customer interaction and satisfaction perspective, measurements of the interface between the individual (the organisational representative) and the customer are a tangible value of product or service worth to the customer.

The real issue, however, is what happens after employee performance has been measured.

3.3. TRADITIONAL USE OF MEASURES

Performance appraisals typically include some standard or goal, a performance period during which a manager presumably monitors employee performance, and a performance review and rating of the employee on various dimensions thought to be critical to the standard or goal. This is why goal setting and planning is so important. If you are going to measure, then measure fairly against agreed measures.

Whereas in the past, performance was measured and then linked directly to reward, these days the process is less punitive. Individual performance is reviewed more frequently, often as a conversation rather than a performance session, with adjustments being made dynamically. The focus is on the contribution the individual is making to organisational success. This means that an individual is viewed increasingly as part of a whole, rather than a single unit.

The general point is that measurement is never an independent undertaking. Measurement needs credibility to be supported. Measurement credibility is obtained by using measures that are concise, ongoing, followed by appropriate actions and information, and are part of an underlying system of measurement. The importance lies in the fact that the measurement system allows for monitoring of performance at different levels in an organisation, and thus for troubleshooting problem areas. In other words, the outputs provide an audit trail whereby faulty processes and individual performance can be corrected.

3.4. BARRIERS TO MEASUREMENT

Gathering performance data on performance issues should not be a tedious task. In essence, the data should be readily available within the job or role spectrum of the individual being evaluated. Closely defined and pinpointed measures are, however, not as common as they should be. People may have sporadically attempted to capture data and not been very successful. Measures need to be part of a holistic measurement system to be effective. The benefits of doing so are substantial, and one cannot afford not to measure and manage performance. There are four main barriers to measurement:

- First, people think that some jobs cannot be measured. Practice in defining and pinpointing performance, on the other hand, reveals that anything can be measured. If it is performance, it can be measured somehow. It is more a question of finding the appropriate approach. With a trained eye, even performances like collaboration, communication, and holding a workshop can be pinpointed and objectively observed. The key question for consideration is: "What specific behaviours will we observe in the execution of this job or role?"
- A second barrier is that people think that measures are hard to work with. However, it is not the measurement that is difficult as much as pinpointing the right behaviours. Once performance is defined in discrete actions, the observation and recording of data are fairly straightforward. A helpful question to ask in this process is: "What do we want the performers to do?"

- The third barrier is traditional thinking, in terms of which it is believed that measurement is an antecedent of punishment. When measurement is used to catch performers who commit some kind of error or perform below standard, the measurements carry negative connotations with them. The way to alter this function of measurement is to apply more positive feedback for correct or desirable behaviours and less negative feedback for errors when using measurement. The real question in mind should be: "What developmental opportunities and programmes should be provided for the individual concerned?"

- Finally, thinking that applying measurement systems is time-consuming and takes time away from other more important issues stops people from using measures of performance. Measures should in fact be as simple as possible (directly job-related) and be added to and refined as is necessary. Establishing a measurement system may take some time, but the long-term benefits of doing so override the initial inconvenience. The fundamental question is: "What are the key performance drivers within this role or job, and what is the simplest way of measuring them?"

3.5. WHAT TO MEASURE

The work in modern organisations is characterised by ongoing and continuous changes in demand. The intense competition that is present in most fields of business forces organisations to be creative and smart in their daily work. This pressure of demand implies that management needs to have a good overview of what is going on inside and outside its organisation, and especially of what the customers want and need.

Measurements can best aid performance accomplishments by moving problem solving and decision making closer to the customers.[43] Flattening the organisational structure by shifting to team-based approaches is a current, prevalent trend that often proves successful in meeting customer demands. Accurate measures of performance are the tools that reveal the need for change and improvement in these flat organisations. These measurements do, however, need to be accurate and appropriate in order to guide the ongoing process. This again underlines the importance of establishing systems of measurement.

There are some problems with systems of measurement:

- It is not always obvious what should be measured.
- Even if it is clear what to measure, it is not always clear how the measurement should be done.
- What seems important to assess may, in many cases, not be easily transferable into numbers.

Questions to be asked in the team measurement process are whether measures should be based on the team as a whole or each member of the team.

- Should the measures focus on processes or performance?
- Should they be qualitative or quantitative in nature, upstream or downstream, and what exactly about performance should be assessed?
- Measurements need to be accurate and reliable to maintain their function and credibility.

Show me the honey!

Once upon a time in Yemen, there were two beekeepers, each of whom had a bee hive. The beekeepers worked for a company called YemBees Ltd. The company's customers loved its honey, and the business aimed to produce more honey than it had the previous year. As a result, each beekeeper was told to produce more honey of the same quality. With different ideas about how to do this, the beekeepers designed different approaches to improve the performance of their hives.

YemBees – beekeeper one

The first beekeeper established a bee performance management approach that measured how many flowers each bee visited. At considerable cost to the beekeeper, an extensive measurement system was created to count the flowers each bee visited. The beekeeper provided feedback for each bee at midseason on his individual performance, but the bees were never told about the hive's goal to produce more honey so that YemBees Ltd. could increase honey sales. The beekeeper created incentives in the form of special awards for the bees who visited the most flowers.

YemBees – beekeeper two

The second beekeeper also established a bee performance management system, but this approach communicated to each bee the goals of the hive – to produce more honey. This beekeeper and his bees measured two aspects of their performance: the amount of nectar each bee brought back to the hive and the amount of honey the hive produced. The performance of each bee and the hive's overall performance were charted and posted on the hive's bulletin board for all bees to see. The beekeeper created a few awards for the bees that gathered the most nectar, but he also established a hive incentive programme that rewarded each bee in the hive based on the hive's production of honey – the more honey produced, the more recognition each bee would receive.

YemBees – performance prediction

What do you think might have happened to each hive at the end of the season when the Queen Bee would report back to each beekeeper?

YemBees beekeeper one at the end of the season

The first beekeeper found that his hive had indeed increased the number of flowers visited, but the amount of honey produced by the hive had dropped. The Queen Bee reported that, because the bees were so busy trying to visit as many flowers as possible, they limited the amount of nectar they would carry, so they could fly faster. Also, because the bees felt they were competing against one another for awards (because only the top performers were recognised), they would not share valuable information with one another, like the location of the flower-filled fields they'd spotted on the way back to the hive that could have helped improve the performance of all the bees. After all was said and done, one of the high-performing bees told the beekeeper that if he'd been told that the real goal was to make more honey rather than to visit more flowers, he would have done his work completely differently.

As the beekeeper handed out the awards to individual bees, unhappy buzzing was heard in the background.

YemBees beekeeper two at the end of the season

The second beekeeper, however, had very different results. Because each bee in his hive was focused on the hive's goal of producing more honey, the bees had concentrated their efforts on gathering more nectar to produce more honey than ever before. The bees worked together to determine the highest nectar-yielding flowers and to create quicker processes for depositing the nectar they'd gathered. They also worked together to help increase the amount of nectar gathered by the poor performers. The Queen Bee of this hive reported that the poor performers either improved their performance or transferred to another hive.

Because the hive had reached its goal, the beekeeper awarded each bee his portion of the hive incentive payment. The beekeeper was also surprised to hear a loud, happy buzz and a jubilant flapping of wings as he rewarded the individual high-performing bees with special recognition.

The moral of this story is:

Design your systems carefully, because they will affect the behaviour of your staff. Measuring and recognising accomplishments rather than activities – and providing feedback for your "worker bees" – can often improve the results of the hive.[44]

3.6. HOW TO USE MEASURES

Measurement is an obvious prerequisite for management, as it allows for identification of performance gaps. Performance measurement links value from the top to the bottom of the organisation. It allows top-driven goals and missions to be linked with operational performance drivers. Ultimately, any measurement system should give a sense of direction as well as insight into what is going on in the organisation. Furthermore, measurement and its backup systems should help in guiding the nature and the quality of the processes that take place within the organisation.

A measurement system is, however, no better than the systems that back it up. Measurements should be the main tool in linking actions to goals. This requires that the right goal first of all be identified. Organisational goal setting and the communication of a clear strategy to achieve those goals are primarily a managerial task. In team-based organisations the teams will also operate with their own goals. These goals need to be aligned both vertically and laterally. Only when goals are clear and appropriate can they yield a clear strategy. Also, the correct measures need to be identified, and they need to be obtained in a manner that secures their internal validity.

3.7. QUANTITATIVE AND QUALITATIVE ISSUES IN MEASURING PERFORMANCE

There are two general ways to measure performance.[45] Behaviours and results can be either counted objectively or judged subjectively.[46]

Quantitative measures entail some form of counting or enumeration which quantifies performance against standards into discrete units that can be measured.[47] This is the preferred method and surpasses judging in reliability (Will the same or similar results be achieved over time?) and validity (Is the attribute being measured the same as the attribute you intended to measure?).[48] Historically, numerical forms of measurement have been preferred, often by financial resources within organisations, as being more objective, and even more exact.

Qualitative measures, on the other hand, require judgement,[49] that is, they entail the subjective aspects of assessing performance.[50] Sound, behaviourally anchored rating systems (BARS) or scales are preferable when performance is measured by judgement. This implies compiling a matrix with solid, descriptive behavioural anchors or criteria for assessing performance.[51] In this case, each number allocated on the performance rating scale is represented by several closely defined behaviours. This allows for accurate measurement that is easy to conduct. The following examples have been constructed as examples of turning "fuzzy" behavioural judgements into objective, numerical measures.

Examples of BARS – the first covers an element of a customer service position or interface, while the other covers that of a receptionist at the front desk of an organisation.

Customer service position – one element

Observable behaviour – criterion	Assigned performance	Numerical value
Having attended to the specific problem and having provided the link between the customer and solution finder, the individual goes the extra mile by following up afterwards with the customer to check that he or she is satisfied with the result and if there are problems that still need to be resolved.	Far exceeds requirements	5
Not only attends to the problems immediately, but also refers them to the correct solution finder for appropriate action and follows up that the solution is implemented.	Exceeds requirements	4
Immediately attends to customer problems, and is pleasant, approachable and helpful.	Meets requirements	3

Observable behaviour – criterion	Assigned performance	Numerical value
Grudgingly attends to customer or client requirements, but is resentful of the intrusion into his or her normal daily priorities.	Meets some requirements	2
Is clearly distracted and resents the intrusion of the customer within the work space. Comes over as bored and inattentive.	Does not meet requirements	1

Receptionist – one element

Observable behaviour – criterion	Assigned performance	Numerical value
Going the extra mile by interfacing with the client after the event to ensure that the client is satisfied with the service he or she has received. Thanks the internal service provider for his or her role in the process.	Far exceeds requirements	5
Follows up after the event to ensure that the appropriate representative has actually solved the client's problem.	Exceeds requirements	4
Answers the call within three to five rings, is pleasant and helpful, referring the client to the appropriate extension/person for assistance. Acts as a pleasant, approachable representative for the organisation.	Meets requirements	3
Takes the call with a view to getting rid of the call as soon as possible, and is surly and unhelpful. Alternatively, is totally unhelpful with the visiting client. Resentful of the intrusion into his or her normal daily priorities.	Meets some requirements	2
Takes his or her time answering the telephone and often loses the call because of either other distractions or priorities. Alternatively, takes time to interact with the client. Comes across as bored and inattentive.	Does not meet requirements	1

On examination, the behavioural descriptor has been isolated and described explicitly as a series of inclusive and progressive steps. This leads to the applied judgement of the assigned performance ranking, and finally to the allocation of a performance number to the observed performance. Again, people do not operate in discrete, distinct little boxes, and so a decision eventually needs to be made as to which box their performance really belongs in. This is always task-specific, and the real danger is that of generalising all perceived behaviour of an individual rather than remaining task- and even role-specific. The situational leadership approach of Hersey, Blanchard and Johnson also requires that a task-specific and not an overall role-specific approach be used in developing and accessing people.[52]

3.8. TYPES OF MEASURES

Measurement itself is a complex arena that requires different perspectives. Sometimes, the weight of the measure itself carries greater importance.

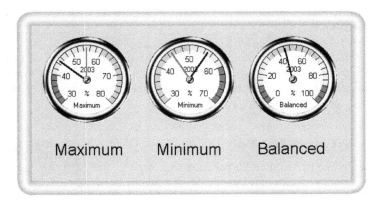

Figure 3.2: The three types of measures

Not all measures are the same. In some areas, performance means increasing or maximising the statistic (eg profitability).

Maximum (Big is Best)	
• Where it is advantageous to maximise the value of the measure • 60–80 ('green') performance band on High Values • E.g. Turnover, market share, etc	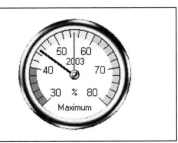

Figure 3.3: Where it is desirable to maximise the measure

In other areas, the desirable attribute would be to minimise the impact of what is going on (e.g. controlling costs).

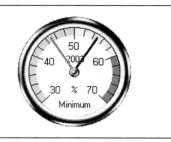

Minimum (Small is Best)

- Where it is advantageous to minimise the value of the measure

- 30–50 ('green') performance band on Low Values

- E.g. Customer complaints, defections

Figure 3.4: Where minimum is best

In a third arena, there would be a balance between minimising or maximising what is going on (eg the trade-off between selling units and achieving marketing margins; or producing large volumes of material/service vis-à-vis achieving quality standards in respect of that material or service).

Balanced (Stabilise)

- Where it is desired to maintain the measure within a range of values

- Either too High or too Low is out of the 32–68 ('green') performance band

- E.g. Training, investment cash flows

Figure 3.5: Where desirable attributes trade-off

3.9. MEASURING TEAM PERFORMANCE

In measuring team performance, the most important point is for the team members to develop an understanding of what is expected of them, and to understand how they are performing according to some pre-set goals or standards. The following is an example of a seven-step model of performance standards for teams:[53]

1. Review existing organisational measures.

2. Balance the integration of measurements (refrain from misguiding teams in their actions).

3. Define the team measurement points.

4. Select accomplishment or process measures as the basis for further team or individual development.

5. Identify individual team member accomplishments that support the team. Team member performance should, however, be measured to provide opportunities for feedback and rewards in cases where this is warranted.

6.   As accomplishments are identified, they should be weighted according to their relative importance, and, subsequently, team and individual performance measures can be developed.

7.   When the different accomplishments and measures have been identified and weighted, one can move on to establish standards for the performances. It is these standards, or goals, that convey performance expectations for the teams and their members.

3.10. HOW TO MEASURE TEAM PERFORMANCE

Many different measurement tools and approaches have been developed which have targeted different aspects of measures. Team measures could be derived either from team results or from the work processes that lead to these results. An integral part of any measurement system, however, is that it be tied to some relevant strategic goal or mission from an organisational perspective. Goals and targets are then set at different levels in an organisation. These goals and mission statements need to be further aligned and refined to serve functional purposes. Similarly, there needs to be alignment between what a team (or individual) actually does and what it should be doing. A solid measurement system is going to provide this kind of valuable information. If teams receive sufficient information and feedback from their data, they are more likely to be able to adapt to the external and internal requirements of performance and eventually surpass competitors in the fight for customers or deliver a world-class service. A prerequisite for this kind of success is that appropriate sub-missions are identified within the organisation as impetus for the teams.

Productivity matrices:

Working with the National Productivity Institute and attending its productivity measure training courses provides a very effective set of matrices that can be used for measurement. Productivity is a very useful metric, and an understanding of the meaning and measurement of productivity is important. This understanding should include the following:

*   Measuring single- and total-factor productivity and establishing the causes of current levels of single-factor productivity.

*   Measuring the quantitative factors that influence productivity, and removing barriers that inhibit labour, material and capital productivity.

*   Understanding the five ways to improve productivity:
    o   effective and efficient resource usage
    o   waste reduction
    o   completing tasks correctly
    o   time management
    o   continuous performance management

3.11. CONCLUSION

Measurement is inextricably linked to performance management. In order to manage performance successfully, one must be able to measure performance. Without this measurement, there is no way of knowing whether performance has improved, declined or remained stable.

The following are the questions and issues that you should focus on for this theme:

*   How best would you effect performance improvement if you do not use measurement?
*   What is the essential difference between qualitative and quantitative measurement systems?
*   What measures will really make a difference, and how?
*   What is the difference between measures applied to private- and public-sector organisations?
*   How can performance measures help with strategic change?
*   How have knowledge management and the information age impacted on the art and science of organisational measurement?

3.12. BIBLIOGRAPHY

Burkes, D. (2016). *How Adobe scrapped its performance review system and why it worked.* Forbes, July, 2016.

Cassell, C & Symon, G. (eds) 1994. *Qualitative methods in organisational research: a practical guide.* London: Sage.

Conger, JA. 1998. Qualitative research as the cornerstone methodology for understanding leadership. *Leadership Quarterly* 9(1) 107-121.

Cunningham, L. 2015. *In big move, Accenture will get rid of annual performance reviews and rankings.* Retrieved from https://www.washingtonpost.com/news/on-leadership/wp/2015/07/21/in-big-move-accenture-will-get-rid-of-annual-performance-reviews-and-rankings/ on 22 February 2017.

De Vos, AS, Strydom, H, Fouche, CB, Poggenpoel, M, Schurink, E & Schurink, W. 2001. *Research at grass roots: a primer for the caring professions.* 3rd impression. Pretoria. Van Schaik Publishers.

Denzin, NK & Lincoln, YS. (eds) 2000. *Handbook of qualitative research.* 2nd ed. Thousand Oaks: Sage.

Denzin, NK & Lincoln, YS. 2005. *The Sage handbook of qualitative research.* 3rd ed. London: Sage.

Fombrun, CJ, Devanna, MA & Tichy, NM. 1998. The human resource management audit, in *The strategic human resource management sourcebook*, edited by LS Baird, CE Schneier & RW Beatty. Amherst, Massachusetts: Human Resource Development Press 250-257.

Ganeshasundaram, R & Henley, N. 2007. "Decision research" correlates directly with better business performance. *Marketing Intelligence & Planning* 25(1) 45-65.

Gummesson. E. 2000. *Qualitative methods in management research.* 2nd ed. Thousand Oaks: Sage. Mason, J. 1996. *Qualitative researching.* London: Sage.

Hersey, P, Blanchard, K & Johnson, DE. 1997. *The management of organisational behaviour.* 7th ed. Upper Saddle River, New Jersey: Prentice-Hall.

Johnson, P & Duberley, J. 2000. *Understanding management research.* Thousand Oaks: Sage.

Leedy PD & Ormrod JE. 2001. *Practical research: planning and design.* 7th ed. Upper Saddle River, New Jersey: Prentice-Hall 155-157.

Nixon, A. 2011. Adapted from *A handbook for measuring employee performance.* Office of Personnel Management, US Government. Retrieved from: http://spectrain.wordpress.com/tag/cross-cultural/.

Patton, MQ. 2002. *Qualitative research and evaluation methods.* 3rd ed. Thousand Oaks: Sage.

Schurink, EM. 2001. Deciding to use a qualitative research approach, in *Research at grass roots* by AS de Vos et al. Pretoria: Van Schaik 239-251.

Zigon. 1995. Zigon Performance Group (ZPG) – retrieved from: http://www.zigonperf.com/.

Endnotes

41. De Vos et al., 2001.
42. Cunningham, 2015.
43. Ganeshasundaram & Henley, 2007.
44. Nixon, 2011.
45. Patton, 2002.
46. Denzin & Lincoln, 2000; Denzin & Lincoln, 2005; Schurink, 2001.
47. Leedy & Ormrod, 2001.
48. Johnson & Duberley, 2000.
49. Conger 1998; Gummesson 2000.
50. Cassell & Symon, 1994.
51. Fombrun, Devanna & Tichy, 1998.
52. Hersey, Blanchard & Johnson, 1997.
53. Zignon, 1995.

4 DEVELOPING AN OUTPUT-DRIVEN PERFORMANCE PLAN

4.1. INTRODUCTION

Before developing rating scales or measurement tools, it is important to know what you are measuring.

Measure what counts – a little story about counting

Once upon a time, a project manager (whose customer service project contained a large information system component) needed high productivity from the programming staff. The project manager (PM) argued long and hard that, in order to run successful projects, managers needed authority. Finally, the PM killed the dragon of the management hierarchy in the organisation and secured the authority to assign work directly to, and reward the work of, the project team members. It was a day of celebration and revelry for every PM in the organisation.

But, in the sober light of the next day, the PM was uncertain as to how to use the new authority. Should every team member get a performance review at the end of each assignment or just at the end of the project? How closely should the work be monitored? After much thought, the PM made a decision.

After some planning, the PM decided to measure programmers' performance according to the number of lines of code they wrote. Linking rewards to this metric, the PM gave out $1 000 end-of-project bonuses.

Not surprisingly, the programmers wrote thousands of lines of code, crushed the metric under a deluge of programming, and earned their bonuses. Equally predictably, the resulting system failed to improve customer service. As a result, the PM lived a miserable, lonely life as a stable sweeper. Worse still, no PMs were ever again granted assignment and reward authority over the people on their project teams.

One of the morals of this story is that the activity of writing code, while certainly necessary, did not really count. What counted was improving customer service. The PM should have counted and rewarded the programmers' measured contribution to the larger customer service achievement rather than the activity of coding. This is achievement-driven project management. Another moral in this story concerns the amount of reward "horsepower" to put behind whatever performance metric we use. Only when we have mastered the art of assigning measured achievements can we dole out large rewards for reaching those achievements.

This chapter is adapted from McLagan International and looks at output-based approaches to performance management, and at how to set output-based goals to ensure that we measure what really counts. This method of performance management is one of my favourites, because it focuses the mind and treats people like mature adults.

4.2. PERFORMANCE MANAGEMENT READINESS

Before you are ready to measure performance, it is essential to understand whether your organisation is ready for the introduction of a performance management system. Implementing a formal system to measure performance can require significant change management, especially if performance was subjectively measured in the past, or was not measured at all. The introduction of a new performance management system can create anxiety and can have reduced impact if the organisation is not ready and not properly prepared. The form below can help you ascertain if your organisation is ready for performance management.

PERFORMANCE MANAGEMENT READINESS QUESTIONNAIRE
SECTION 1: CHANGE MISSION AND STRATEGY

Legend: **N** = No   **U** = Uncertain
DN = Definitely not   **YD** = Yes, definitely
Y = Yes

Number	QUESTIONS Please indicate the extent to which you agree or disagree with each of these statements by placing an **X** in the appropriate space to indicate your view.	DN	N	U	Y	YD
1.1	Do you understand the purpose of implementing a PMS?					
1.2	Are you familiar with the content of a PMS?					
1.3	Do you know what your role is in implementing a PMS?					
1.4	Does the company have a specific strategy to manage the sources of resistance to change?					

SECTION 2: EXTERNAL ENVIRONMENT

Legend: **N** = No   **U** = Uncertain
DN = Definitely not   **YD** = Yes, definitely
Y = Yes

Number	QUESTIONS Please indicate the extent to which you agree or disagree with each of these statements by placing an **X** in the appropriate space to indicate your view.	DN	N	U	Y	YD
2.1	Do you think that your customer base will support the implementation of a PMS?					
2.2	Will the implementation of a PMS take into account the latest market trends?					
2.3	Will the implementation of a PMS take into account technological developments?					

SECTION 3: CHANGE LEADERSHIP

Legend: **N** = No   **U** = Uncertain
DN = Definitely not   **YD** = Yes, definitely
Y = Yes

Number	QUESTIONS Please indicate the extent to which you agree or disagree with each of these statements by placing an **X** in the appropriate space to indicate your view.	DN	N	U	Y	YD
3.1	Does top management have a clear vision of the change to be made, eg implementation of a PMS?					
3.2	Do all the members of top management support the implementation of a PMS?					
3.3	Do employees have confidence in top management's ability to manage implementation of change initiatives?					

SECTION 3: CHANGE LEADERSHIP

Legend:
DN = Definitely not
Y = Yes

N = No

U = Uncertain
YD = Yes, definitely

Number	QUESTIONS Please indicate the extent to which you agree or disagree with each of these statements by placing an **X** in the appropriate space to indicate your view.	DN	N	U	Y	YD
3.4	Does top management show commitment to the change initiatives within the organisation?					
3.5	Does top management always communicate the implementation of change initiatives to the employees?					
3.6	Are there people to drive the change process in the organisation?					

SECTION 4: ORGANISATIONAL CULTURE SUPPORTIVE OF CHANGE

Legend:
DN = Definitely not
Y = Yes

N = No

U = Uncertain
YD = Yes, definitely

Number	QUESTIONS Please indicate the extent to which you agree or disagree with each of these statements by placing an **X** in the appropriate space to indicate your view.	DN	N	U	Y	YD
4.1	Is the working environment safe for making suggestions for improvements?					
4.2	Are the employees' new ideas considered for implementation of any change initiative?					
4.3	Are the employees encouraged to make suggestions regarding the implementation of a PMS?					

SECTION 5: ORGANISATIONAL CULTURE SUPPORTIVE OF CHANGE

Legend: **N** = No   **U** = Uncertain
DN = Definitely not   **YD** = Yes, definitely
Y = Yes

Number	QUESTIONS Please indicate the extent to which you agree or disagree with each of these statements by placing an **X** in the appropriate space to indicate your view.	DN	N	U	Y	YD
5.1	Is the structure of your company flexible enough to allow changes?					
5.2	Are the company policies flexible enough to accommodate a PMS?					
5.3	Is the structure of your company conducive to the implementation of a PMS?					

SECTION 6: CHANGE MANAGEMENT PRACTICES

Legend: **N** = No   **U** = Uncertain
DN = Definitely not   **YD** = Yes, definitely
Y = Yes

Number	QUESTIONS Please indicate the extent to which you agree or disagree with each of these statements by placing an **X** in the appropriate space to indicate your view.	DN	N	U	Y	YD
6.1	Is the implementation of any change initiative always championed by the most influential people within the organisation?					
6.2	Is the expected time period to make the change always realistic?					
6.3	Are the change initiatives within the organisation always well planned?					
6.4	Are all the components of the business considered in compiling the change initiatives?					

SECTION 6: CHANGE MANAGEMENT PRACTICES

Legend: **N** = No   **U** = Uncertain
DN = Definitely not   **YD** = Yes, definitely
Y = Yes

Number	QUESTIONS Please indicate the extent to which you agree or disagree with each of these statements by placing an **X** in the appropriate space to indicate your view.	DN	N	U	Y	YD
6.5	Are the employees who are affected by the change involved in drafting the change plans?					
6.6	Are the employees committed to the change initiatives within the organisation?					
6.7	Do the employees receive regular feedback on change initiatives being planned, eg PMS implementation?					
6.8	Are the employees equipped to manage the changes taking place?					
6.9	Do the change initiatives within the organisation consist of well-coordinated interventions?					

SECTION 7: CHANGE-RELATED SYSTEMS

Legend: **N** = No   **U** = Uncertain
DN = Definitely not   **YD** = Yes, definitely
Y = Yes

Number	QUESTIONS Please indicate the extent to which you agree or disagree with each of these statements by placing an **X** in the appropriate space to indicate your view.	DN	N	U	Y	YD
7.1	Does the company's remuneration system support the change initiatives within the organisation?					

SECTION 7: CHANGE-RELATED SYSTEMS

Legend: **N** = No   **U** = Uncertain
DN = Definitely not   **YD** = Yes, definitely
Y = Yes

Number	QUESTIONS Please indicate the extent to which you agree or disagree with each of these statements by placing an **X** in the appropriate space to indicate your view.	DN	N	U	Y	YD
7.2	Are sufficient human resources allocated to manage the change initiatives within the organisation?					
7.3	Are sufficient financial resources allocated to the change initiatives within the organisation?					

SECTION 8: WORK UNIT CLIMATE

Legend: **N** = No   **U** = Uncertain
DN = Definitely not   **YD** = Yes, definitely
Y = Yes

Number	QUESTIONS Please indicate the extent to which you agree or disagree with each of these statements by placing an **X** in the appropriate space to indicate your view.	DN	N	U	Y	YD
8.1	Do the people in your work unit encourage one another to support the change initiatives within the organisation, such as the implementation of a PMS?					
8.2	Do people in your work unit perceive change as positive?					
8.3	Are people selected to act as change agents fully trained?					
8.4	Is counselling always available to people who suffer from the emotional effects of a change initiative?					

SECTION 9: JOB/TASK REQUIREMENTS

Legend:
DN = Definitely not   **N** = No   **U** = Uncertain
Y = Yes   **YD** = Yes, definitely

Number	QUESTIONS Please indicate the extent to which you agree or disagree with each of these statements by placing an **X** in the appropriate space to indicate your view.	DN	N	U	Y	YD
9.1	Will it be easy for people to make changes to the content of their jobs when a PMS is implemented?					
9.2	Do people receive training to cope with their new job requirements?					
9.3	Will people cope with increased job variety?					
9.4	Will people be able to reach their full potential when a PMS is implemented?					
9.5	Will change bring about new challenges in people's jobs?					
9.6	Do the managers have the necessary skills to manage their teams through the change initiative, eg implementation of a PMS?					

SECTION 10: MOTIVATION TO CHANGE

Legend:
DN = Definitely not   **N** = No   **U** = Uncertain
Y = Yes   **YD** = Yes, definitely

Number	QUESTIONS Please indicate the extent to which you agree or disagree with each of these statements by placing an **X** in the appropriate space to indicate your view.	DN	N	U	Y	YD
10.1	Will people be committed to achieving the objectives of a PMS?					

SECTION 10: MOTIVATION TO CHANGE

Legend:
DN = Definitely not
Y = Yes

N = No

U = Uncertain
YD = Yes, definitely

Number	QUESTIONS Please indicate the extent to which you agree or disagree with each of these statements by placing an **X** in the appropriate space to indicate your view.	DN	N	U	Y	YD
10.2	Do employees believe that the implementation of a PMS will improve the performance of the organisation?					
10.3	Do employees believe that the implementation of a PMS will be beneficial to them?					
10.4	Are people looking forward to the implementation of a PMS?					

SECTION 11: PERSONAL IMPACT OF CHANGE

Legend:
DN = Definitely not
Y = Yes

N = No

U = Uncertain
YD = Yes, definitely

Number	QUESTIONS Please indicate the extent to which you agree or disagree with each of these statements by placing an **X** in the appropriate space to indicate your view.	DN	N	U	Y	YD
11.1	Do most people believe that the implementation of a PMS will have a positive effect on their earnings?					
11.2	Do people openly talk about their fears associated with the implementation of a PMS?					
11.3	Will people's power networks be disturbed during the change initiative?					
11.4	Will the implementation of a PMS improve relationships among staff members and with their supervisors?					

SECTION 12: EMOTIONAL IMPACT OF CHANGE

Legend: **N** = No   **U** = Uncertain
DN = Definitely not   **YD** = Yes, definitely
Y = Yes

Number	QUESTIONS Please indicate the extent to which you agree or disagree with each of these statements by placing an **X** in the appropriate space to indicate your view.	DN	N	U	Y	YD
12.1	Is the implementation of a PMS viewed as fair towards employees?					
12.2	Is the implementation of a PMS viewed as an additional stress factor at work?					
12.3	Do employees feel that a new PMS would be different from previous unsuccessful efforts?					

SECTION 13: CHANGE PROCESS

Legend: **N** = No   **U** = Uncertain
DN = Definitely not   **YD** = Yes, definitely
Y = Yes

Number	QUESTIONS Please indicate the extent to which you agree or disagree with each of these statements by placing an **X** in the appropriate space to indicate your view.	DN	N	U	Y	YD
13.1	**Willingly** (choose to) be part of a new change initiative.					
13.2	**Willingly** (choose to) change the way you work because of the change process.					
13.3	**Willingly** (choose to) focus on improving the current situation rather than pursuing the change process.					
13.4	**Willingly** (choose to) take the blame when the change process or elements thereof fail.					
13.5	**Willingly** (choose to) provide support for the remainder of the change process.					

Source: Roodt & Kinnear[54]

4.3. GOAL SETTING – WHAT DOES THE CUSTOMER WANT?

In organisations that are competing for customer attention, the most effective performance goals focus on **outputs** rather than activities, levels of behaviour, or even results. Why? Because, when you are customer-focused, the following goal-setting questions are asked: "What must I provide my customers with in order to ensure that we achieve our business results?" Or, "What products, services, information, or processes do my customers expect?" This is an output question, not an activity question. An output focus in performance goals fulfils the five important functions of goals. The output focus:

*   clarifies what individuals must contribute in order to help the business achieve its strategies.
*   connects individuals with their customers and the customers' quality requirements
*   focuses communication concerning the individual's responsibilities.
*   helps individuals think of themselves as "a business within the business".
*   sets the stage for creating the future (ie changing other behaviours and activities to provide the customer with the appropriate product or service).

Outputs are better focuses for goals than activities and behaviour because it is outputs that the customer wants. If you set activities as performance goals, you may constrain the creativity and continuous improvement that are so essential for higher levels of quality, productivity, and work fulfilment. For example, there is a significant difference between a goal of "sweeping the floor" and one of producing "a clean floor". The former is an activity which does not really represent what the customer wants (a clean floor). Nor does it take into consideration that a clean floor can be accomplished by many means: using doormats, vacuuming, installing air cleaners, or mopping, for example. By focusing on outputs, you specify the ends and not the means, thereby leaving room for innovation in how the ends are accomplished.

Outputs also broaden the focus of goals beyond results. In a customer-focused approach to goals, financial or quantitative results that are valuable to the organisation may be outputs for which individuals are responsible. But, in a customer-focused orientation, focusing on results exclusively isn't enough. To gain a business result, such as "realising a one-third increase in profits" or "doubling the size of the company in two years", you must satisfy your customers – provide them with the products and services that bind them to you. That brings you back to outputs.

4.4. UNDERSTANDING KEY PERFORMANCE AREAS (KPAs)

KPAs are the four to six short statements that describe the areas (or categories of outputs) that are essential for success in a particular role. The scope (depth and breadth) of the KPAs will vary, depending on the seniority of the role that is being described. For example, at a senior level, the manager may be held responsible for the **marketing** of a product (product availability, price, place and promotion), while, at a more operational level, an employee may be held responsible for **selling** the same product (sales volumes).

KPAs do not describe the tasks that are performed within the role (tasks are part of the inputs to a role) or the outputs needed by the organisation. KPAs also do not indicate "how well" or "how much" or "when" or what standard of performance is expected. The quantification happens when objectives are contracted between the manager and employee.

The relative importance of different KPAs can be indicated by weighting the KPA. A percentage is attached to each KPA to indicate its importance. All the KPAs together should add up to 100 per cent.

4.5. ADDING KEY PERFORMANCE INDICATORS (KPIs) TO THE KEY PERFORMANCE AREAS (KPAs)

KPIs are the measurement areas used for indicating performance. One KPA might have two or three KPIs, and another might have only one.

4.5.1. Contracting concrete outputs

An output is "something towards which effort is directed". As such, outputs are very specific and measurable, and are linked to KPIs. When all the outputs for a particular KPI are "added up", they describe what the incumbent must do to be successful in respect of a particular KPA.

Outputs must adhere to the SMART rule ("SMART" is an acronym for **Specific, Measurable, Actionable, Realistic,** and **Time-bound**):

- **Specific:** does the output say **what** must be done?
- **Measurable:** does the output specify a **quantity** or **how well** the actions need to be executed? "Measurable" refers to the standard to which the actions need to be completed.
- **Actionable:** does the output state what the individual must do to achieve the "what"? To ensure that the output is "actionable", begin the sentence with a **verb**. This ensures an action orientation to the objective right from the start.
- **Realistic:** are the outputs, time frames, and quantities specified within the scope of the expertise of the person with whom the output is contracted? Can it be done?
- **Time-bound:** does it say **when** the outputs will be due? If required, does it specify interim checkpoints and milestones?

An output must therefore:

- specify the detail about the **output** required
- **quantify** what you want
- set a **due date**

Examples of action words that can be used when crafting actionable outputs

Adjust	Align	Analyse	Assemble	Assist
Balance	Build	Blend		
Check	Change	Control	Compile	
Deliver	Design	Distribute		
Evaluate	Establish	Employ	Examine	
Find	Formulate	File	Finalise	
Generate				
Handle	Help			
Inspect	Install	Instruct	Implement	
Launch	Lead	Locate		
Maintain	Manage	Make	Measure	Monitor
Negotiate				
Obtain	Organise			
Participate	Perform	Plan	Provide	
Report	Resolve	Restrict		
Select	Schedule	Submit	Service	
Track	Train	Test	Transfer	
Update	Untangle	Utilise		
Validate	Verify			

Example of KPA application

KPA	Weighting	KPI	OUTPUT	DELIVERED BY TO CUSTOMER
Marketing	50%	• Increase in market share • Marketing plan	• Increase market share by 5% • New marketing plan developed and in use by regions	31 March 20xx to Marketing Director/CEO 31 January 20xx to CEO
Remuneration policy	50%	• Board approval and implemented	• Tax structuring of packages implemented	28 February to Board/ Finance Director

4.6. PRODUCING OUTPUT-ORIENTED GOALS – THE SIX QUESTIONS

To guide and manage performance, the key concern is thus "what to provide the customer with so that we can accomplish the business' results **and** create a strong foundation for future business success". Focusing on **outputs** is the nucleus of the customer-focused approach to performance goals.

To produce output-oriented goals – that is, goals that focus on the customer – you must continuously ask and answer these six questions:

• Who are my **customers**?

• What will be the **context** of my work?

• What **outputs** will I provide my customers with?

• What are my customers' **quality requirements**?

• What **indicators** (or measures) of quality will be used?

• What **competencies** will I develop to provide outputs that satisfy customer requirements?

These six questions are important to the customer-focused approach to goal setting for the following reasons:

• It is important to know your **customers** because, ultimately, they set the standards for your work.

• If you forecast the future work **context** you will have a head start on any changes that will affect your work.

• Setting goals in terms of **what you will deliver** (outputs) rather than **how** you will get the work done (activities) gives you freedom to innovate. This way, you can keep your eye on the ball (outputs), not on the bat (activities).

- When you strive for **quality**, not minimum standards, you will become your customers' "preferred supplier". You'll also help your organisation to stay competitive and keep personal challenge in your work.

- Knowing the **indicators** or measures of quality helps you see when you've met your goals. These indicators can be quantitative or qualitative. Quantitative (numerical) measures aren't always possible or cost-effective. You must also use more subjective indicators such as customer opinions and perceptions to evaluate your progress.

- You must know what competencies (knowledge, skills, and other personal qualities) you will need to develop in order to excel. Your continuous development is important to your performance – and to your continued fulfilment through work.

You should, at any time, be able to answer these six questions about your work and your role. You should also be able to list the goals you're working toward at any time – or your written list should be within easy reach. To help you with the process of goal setting, the rest of this section explains the six questions in detail.

Question 1: Who are my customers?

Customers are the people who use or receive the products, services, information, or processes you produce, provide, or deliver.

Everyone has customers. Examples of customers include:

- the end users who pay the organisation for its products and services
- someone in the department down the passage
- your colleagues
- the people who work for you.

Customers can be groups, such as "end users" or "the accounting department", or individuals, such as a specific person in the organisation. Keep in mind that these individuals or groups are those to whom you deliver or for whom you provide products, services, information, or processes.

Question 2: What will be the context of my work?

The context of your work consists of two major components:

- the future forces that will affect your organisation and your job
- your job mission.

Future forces are the changing influence on your job. They may include changes in:

- technology
- political, social, or economic environment or trends
- the organisation's goals or structure
- government regulations.

Question 2: What will be the context of my work?

Forces that will affect how you do your job can be anything from new equipment to changing product emphases, to organisational restructuring.

Your job mission is a statement of:

* your job scope
* the business results you influence
* why your job exists.

It describes the value you add to the organisation.

Question 3: What outputs will I provide for my customers?

Outputs are what you produce or provide for, or deliver to, your customers. Outputs are:

* products
* services
* information
* processes

Examples: products or product components, services or service components, strategies, analyses, decisions, designs, or financial or quantitative results. If you are responsible for the quality of processes used, processes may be your outputs too.

Outputs are stated as nouns and end-states, not verbs or activities. You have a good outputs list if it:

* focuses on what your key customers will receive from you
* reflects your future context and supports the strategies and goals of the business
* is within your authority to provide or influence
* includes important support for others
* includes task force or ad hoc, as well as core job, work

If you are an individual contributor, your outputs are what you directly provide – with or without support from fellow team members.

If you are a manager, your outputs include broad outputs of the group you manage, functional outputs you may provide as an individual contributor, and managerial outputs such as budgets and strategies.

Outputs versus overall results

Outputs are the products, services, information, processes, or specific quantitative or financial results you provide in order **to achieve** overall results such as satisfied customers, a profitable business, or increased market share. Overall results are indicators that you've met specific needs. They are not the purpose of the business.

What role, then, do overall business results play in customer-focused goals? Consider any results for which you are responsible as outputs that you provide for stakeholders (a key customer group).

You may have an output of financial results, or one of market position. In customer-focused goals, customer satisfaction pervades the process. It is what you get if you achieve your goals. So are financial results, but the latter are a major deliverable to a special class of customers: the shareholders whose investments keep you in business. Thus, they should be focused on separately in your goal-setting process.

To answer this third goal-setting question, "What outputs will I provide for my customers?":

•   Talk to your customers.

•   Look at things from their perspective.

•   Ask what they would like to receive from you that has value for them.

•   Think of outputs as nouns (functioning water pumps), not verbs (to repair pumps); as end-states (managerial candidates), not activities (to train employees).

Goals that stress activities may actually inhibit innovation and quality performance, because they often don't encourage "finding a better way"; nor do they facilitate meeting ad hoc, surprise requirements. Goals that stress outputs are more flexible. For example:

•   If a teenager sees his job as "watering the garden" (an activity), he will probably focus solely on the act of watering. On the other hand, if he is responsible for producing "a healthy garden" (an output), he'll be more alert for cues from the garden about what it needs. He will do what's necessary for the garden's health, whether it be weeding, fertilising, watering, irrigating, or eliminating insects.

•   If a manager sees her job as "training people" (an activity), she may be satisfied to send them to classes. If, on the other hand, her responsibility is to produce "managerial candidates" (an output), she'll be concerned that her people actually acquire the knowledge and skills that will make them good candidates. This approach may require developing new training materials, providing developmental opportunities on the job, finding self-study materials, sending people to classes, testing competencies, coaching, or any number of methods that may produce the final output: managerial candidates.

•   If an engineer sees his job as "drafting" (an activity), he may measure his effectiveness in terms of work quantity. If he sees it as producing "accepted designs" (an output), he'll be prepared to vary his techniques and develop the relationships necessary to ensure that his designs meet the customers' specifications.

Thus the third goal-setting question is, "What outputs will I provide for my customers?" In other words, what products, services, information, or processes will you deliver to your key customers during the next year? These may take several forms:

•   **General, ongoing outputs**, such as:
   o   technical advice
   o   solutions to problems
   o   contracts
   o   performance feedback
   o   sales presentations
   o   quantitative or financial results

- **Special, time-bound outputs that support current business initiatives**, such as:

  o the 20xx business strategy

  o a quality-improvement programme

  o the packaging design for a particular product

  o contracts for a specific project

- **Outputs that support others' outputs**, such as:

  o recommendations to the Communications Task Force

  o input to New Sales Strategy Report

  o new processes that will enable work to flow more smoothly, with a better use of resources (eg, a new meeting process or a new customer complaint-handling process).

Question 4: What are my customers' quality requirements?

Identify and, if necessary, negotiate with the customer, each output's quality requirements. Customers do have requirements, although they may not articulate them until they've received the product or service and found it to be inadequate. It's in their best interest and in yours to know what the requirements are **before** you begin your work. Don't assume that you know what they are without asking.

People who frequently talk to their customers may feel that they can establish quality requirements without having a special conversation with the customer or customer representatives. But expectations, needs, and competition change frequently in today's environment. Even people who have close and frequent conversations with their customers can benefit from a periodic discussion of requirements. For others, this step in goal setting provides an opportunity to clarify and shape customer expectations.

Quality requirements take three main forms:

- Quantitative

- Technical

- Interpersonal and subjective

The following example shows quality for all three forms:

Quality requirements for office building	
Quantitative	• Is completed within 12 months • Costs less than 20 million
Technical	• Is expandable • Provides effective climate control • Has totally reliable mechanical systems • Fits in architecturally with surrounding buildings • Has electrical systems and layout support for advanced office technology

Quality requirements for office building	
Interpersonal and subjective	• Attracts people from all parts of the community • Has the support of the town council • Has an attractive meeting space (or meeting spaces) • Is appropriate for small, professional businesses

---

Question 5: What indicators (or measures) of quality will be used?

Indicators show whether the quality requirements have been met. They are the source of feedback about how well you've met the quality requirements. Sometimes, they are the means by which you will be evaluated.

You will not always have indicators for every quality requirement. You should list indicators only if:

• measures, such as budgets or specifications, must be used

• you think there might be a disagreement (or confusion) with your manager or customers about the quality of your output.

Indicators may involve direct measurement (such as a thermometer or survey) or more subtle cues or subjective perceptions (such as feedback or feelings). Indicators may be:

• instruments that directly measure your output

• survey data

• formal and informal feedback

• indirect, subtle cues or perceptions.

In some forms of goal setting, "If you can't measure it, it can't be a goal". In customer-focused goal setting, the **customer**, not measurability, determines performance goals. If the customer has a subjective requirement that is difficult to measure, it is still a requirement, even though you won't be able to count it, weigh it, index it, or otherwise measure it.

Quantitative measures are not the only way to know if you've met the customer's requirements. You can tell by looking at many **sources of feedback** or **indicators**. Some indicators are formal, such as customer surveys, while others are informal and anecdotal, such as voluntary feedback by co-workers.

Some common types of indicators or sources of feedback include the following:

• **Tools** that directly measure outputs – such as sales statistics, quality statistics, or financial ratios.

• **Formal questionnaires** or **surveys** that ask customers to evaluate the quality of products, services, information, or processes (ie the outputs).

• **Systematic feedback conversations** in meetings designed to get feedback from key customers.

- **Informal feedback** that customers volunteer or that is requested daily as opportunities arise.
- **Indirect, often subtle cues**, such as changes in the customer's patterns of interaction, increased signs of tension in the relationship, or increased use of other suppliers.

Clearly, some of these indicators are less objective, systematic, and certain than others. But, in today's rapidly changing times, it is not possible or cost-effective to use rigorous formal measurements on everything. Informal, ad hoc indicators such as random feedback may be enough to keep you on track and your customers happy.

Question 6: What *competencies* will I develop to provide outputs that satisfy customer requirements?

Competencies are identified behaviours, knowledge, skills, and abilities that directly and positively impact the success of employees and organisations.

Competencies can be objectively measured, enhanced, and improved through coaching and learning opportunities.

Examples of competencies that are commonly linked to satisfying customer requirements include:

- information-seeking
- impact and influence
- customer service orientation
- organisational awareness
- teamwork and cooperation
- relationship-building
- initiative
- interpersonal understanding

Indicators that could be linked to these competencies include the following:

- Listens and responds effectively to customer questions.
- Resolves customer problems to the customer's satisfaction.
- Respects all internal and external customers.
- Uses a team approach when dealing with customers.
- Follows up in order to evaluate customer satisfaction.
- Measures customer satisfaction effectively.
- Commits to exceeding customer expectations.

4.7. BRINGING YOUR GOALS TO LIFE

The six goal-setting questions can guide and focus your thinking about what you will accomplish, for whom, what competencies you'll need, and how you'll know when you've succeeded. But setting goals is useless unless you act to turn your goals into realised outputs and results. You can facilitate this process and help ensure your success if you take into account the following Four A's:

Alignment

Connect your goals with the organisation's major business strategies and your customers' needs.

Agreement

Gain the acknowledgement of your manager, customers, co-workers, and others that they will support your goals.

Adjustment

Fine-tune and change your goals on an ongoing basis to take advantage of opportunities, to stimulate continuous improvement, and to adjust to new forces and priorities.

Accountability

Take ownership of your goals and accept responsibility for managing your performance.

An example of an individual goals worksheet follows.

E XAMPLE OF INDIVIDUAL GOALS WORKSHEET Individual goals worksheet **Training Manager**		
OUTPUTS*	**QUALITY REQUIREMENTS**	**INDICATORS/ MEASURES**
What are the key end products, services, information, and processes you will provide during the next performance period?	**What would it look like to the customer if it were excellent?**	**What evidence or sources of feedback (both tangible and intangible) will tell you if you've been successful in meeting your quality requirements?**
Needs analysis (Line management, employees)	Appropriate and sufficient information obtained to analyse needs All personnel covered Accurate identification of problems and opportunities Business orientation	Needs analysis document
Training plan (Line management, employees)	Training plan is practical and meets customer's identified needs Training plan discussed with relevant customers and approved Training plan technically sound Linked to business objectives	Training plan Customer feedback

EXAMPLE OF INDIVIDUAL GOALS WORKSHEET		
Individual goals worksheet **Training Manager**		
OUTPUTS*	**QUALITY REQUIREMENTS**	**INDICATORS/ MEASURES**
Training programmes/ interventions design (Line management, employees)	Design supports Company X: business plan Design supports PM, company mission, values and culture Content is up to date and relevant to objectives	
Programme materials (Line management, employees)	Learning resources and methods are appropriate A plan for evaluation is included Meet both time and budget constraints Meet programme objectives Are flexible – training can tailor material to learner's needs Easy to use Content can easily be transferred/linked to work situation Meet Company X: T & D division standards of professionalism	

4.8. PRACTICAL EXAMPLE

Well-written outputs and performance indicators take the "pain" out of the dreaded performance assessment process. With this approach, one should just rate if the output was achieved or not. This is a bit like landing a plane – one can either land a plane, or one can't. There is no mark, such as 57 per cent, for landing planes.

An example of an output-driven performance contract follows.

OUTPUTS/ DELIVERABLE	CONDITIONS/ QUALITY REQUIREMENTS	HOW WILL WE KNOW/ INDICATORS	WHO HAS INPUT?	DELIVERED BY: TO CUSTOMER
1. Total package and tax structuring of packages implemented	- Legal - Payroll can handle it	Board sign-off and implemented	Auditor and Tax Manager	28 February to Board or Finance Director

OUTPUTS/ DELIVERABLE	CONDITIONS/ QUALITY REQUIREMENTS	HOW WILL WE KNOW/ INDICATORS	WHO HAS INPUT?	DELIVERED BY: TO CUSTOMER
2. Performance management system implemented	- Controlled and owned by Line managers - Process developed and manuals provided - All managers undergo training - Easy to use	Board sign-off and implemented	Line Managers and Consultants	30th June to Operations Director
3. Debtors days reduced to 45 days	- Debtors days reduced from 60 to 45 - Process developed and in place - All debtors clerks undergo training - No customer complaints	Management accounts	Finance Manager and Debtors Clerk	30th June to Finance Director
4. New finance system implemented to track EVA	- Compatible with current system in place - "Real time" queries can be done	CEO sign-off and implemented	IT Manager, Finance Director and CEO	31 December to CEO

4.9. CONCLUSION

An output-driven performance plan ensures that the results of performance measurement are useful. The focus is on results and not necessarily on what you do to achieve those results. Customers are not usually concerned with **how** you meet their expectations. Their interest is in having their expectations met – output, not process!

4.10. BIBLIOGRAPHY

Roodt, G & Kinnear, C. 2007. *Change Readiness Inventory (CRI) manual*. Johannesburg: Jopie van Rooyen & Partners SA (Pty) Ltd.

McLagan International. 2006. *Outputs, not activities*. Unpublished paper.

Endnotes

54.   Roodt & Kinnear, 2007.

5 PERFORMANCE APPRAISAL

5.1. INTRODUCTION

The performance appraisal is the formal process whereby managers appraise, and provide feedback to, employees regarding their performance. It is also a process of identifying, measuring and developing human performance in the organisation. The main objectives of performance evaluation are to:

- focus performance in the direction of the organisation's vision, mission, values, and critical success factors
- provide employees with feedback on their performance
- strengthen the interviewer-interviewee relationship by providing an opportunity for communication
- provide a basis on which to reward employees
- provide the organisation with current data for use in its planning efforts
- develop each staff member in terms of his or her potential, effort, strengths, weaknesses, personal objectives, and the opportunities available in the organisation

The performance appraisal is carried out for each employee by the manager to whom the employee reports. All employees need to prepare for their appraisal in order to derive maximum benefit from the process.

5.2. PHILOSOPHY OF PERFORMANCE APPRAISAL

5.2.1. The individual and the organisation

The context of performance appraisal in relation to the organisation as a whole is important to understand. Each employee should know that his or her own needs and objectives will be taken into account alongside those of the organisation. The planned performance of each individual should be aligned with the overall objectives of the department and those of the organisation. Schematically, this may be shown as follows:

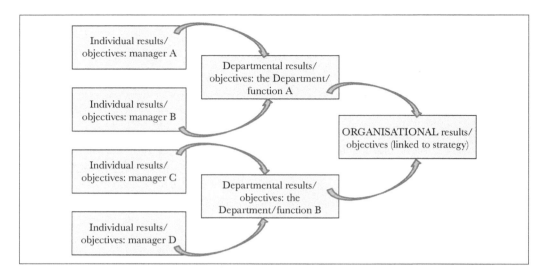

Figure 5.1: The alignment of individual, departmental and organisational results

5.2.2. Objectivity versus judgement

The rater's opinions are made more objective by adherence to standard procedures surrounding a manageable number of performance dimensions. Bias is mitigated, to some extent, through training procedures and the use of a standardised reference document.

A further safeguard against unfair judgement lies in the establishment of an approach of ongoing assessment. Informed feedback and coaching enable manager and employee to establish a relationship of constructive appraisal and discussion of performance improvement over a period of time. This will create the correct environment for the intermittent, formal evaluations and will prevent unpleasant surprises and resentful reactions that are often encountered.

The role of the Human Resources (HR) department must also be emphasised during the appraisal process. As a further safeguard against unfair judgement, the HR department will be responsible for reviewing appraisal forms and dealing with issues where parties to the appraisal would like to question the outcomes of the process.

5.2.3. Job profiles and objectives

Objective evaluation implies that accurate job profiles exist and are available to each manager while appraising employees. The job profile should be used in pointing out to each employee how he or she fared in relation to stated duties and objectives (best presented as key performance areas). The organisation's efforts at ensuring that energy is correctly spent on goal-directed actions should serve to foster the management by objectives approach at the level of individual performance.

This approach should provide an accord between manager and employee in respect of what is expected in the job, what standards have to be met, and what objectives are to be set for the following:

- The work itself, and the improvement of the employee's performance and development of knowledge, skills and attitudes.
- The key performance areas to be achieved and the activities associated with the achievement of these key performance areas. Key performance areas should focus on the ongoing or long-term activities relating to the position. Measurements represented as key performance indicators state the standard of performance required for competence on the job. Inherent competencies or skills and knowledge are included in the job profile and allow for identification of specific training needs during the appraisal process.
- The objectives for the next appraisal, which should list specific actions to be taken in the immediate future (ie the specified period ending with the next appraisal). This relates to one or more of the key performance areas as set out in the job description. The objectives for the next appraisal should set a standard or measure, together with completion dates.

5.2.4. Considerations before implementation

The system of performance appraisal is designed to improve the management of employees and should therefore not be used mechanistically or become a meaningless chore. It is important to ensure that the procedure does not take unnecessarily long to apply or is cumbersome and therefore unwelcome.

Each organisation's managers should, therefore, implement the system to suit their situation. Flexibility is essential, but so is adherence to the basic principles of performance appraisal. Clear communication and the motivation of people through the setting of attainable, but challenging, objectives should also be taken into account. Points to consider are the following:

- Time intervals between appraisals. Salary reviews take place annually, while people-development actions and feedback on performance should occur at least as frequently, but preferably every six months. This makes for timeous course corrections, shorter meetings, less chance of misunderstanding, and more reliable overall assessments.
- Training all employees in the appraisal procedures, in effective interviewing techniques, in handling comments, and in the tasks of planning and motivating. This is essential for the system to function properly.
- The levels to which rating and interviewing tasks can be delegated.
- The raters' standards or "strictness" in their appraisals should reflect the standard of performance normally expected from employees in the particular position or grade.

Chandler's "Fatal Flaws" and "Fundamental Shifts" of Performance Management

Chandler's[55] book on *How performance management is killing performance* highlights some of the mind shifts that are taking place in the area of performance management today. The primary shift is away from the static, negative, demoralising once a year performance review, to a developmental process that is more suited to building people in the new world of work. One size does not fit all – each performance management system must suit the workplace for which it is designed.

Chandler sets out 8 fatal flaws of performance management, and 8 shifts that are necessary to significantly move the performance management dial.

The 8 fatal flaws are summarised as follows:

1. Traditional performance management systems can actually depress performance – they may be so demoralising and have such unclear links to activities, that people may not be able to adapt or improve their behaviour.
2. The performance management process is often about the manager being a judge, and the employee sitting in judgement. There is little to no room for frank, open and constructive discussion.
3. There is a focus on the negative rather than the positive.
4. The person is under the spotlight rather than the organisation and structures around the person.
5. Objectively evaluating the person is almost impossible with forced rankings and a diverse organisation.
6. Ranking systems can discourage honest feedback.
7. Rankings can pit people against each other rather than encouraging team work.
8. Traditional performance management incentivises people with monetary rewards while people are increasingly motivated by a wide variety of factors, not just money.

So what has to change?

Chandler lists the following 8 fundamental shifts that are required:

1. The performance management process must be open and honest. Conversations should be clear and open; don't keep information from people.
2. Allow employees to own their careers – they should feel empowered to develop and drive their own careers.
3. Focus on the future – what Chandler calls a performance **preview**, not performance **review**.
4. Allow managers and teams to develop their own performance management processes – they are more likely to "own" them and they know the activities and objectives of the team better than the team managers.
5. Encourage managers and executives to have talent discussions, discuss objectives, and provide open feedback.
6. The objective of performance management should be empowerment not policing – treat poorly performing employees individually and as the exception, but let the process unfold in the team as normal.
7. Think about introducing team objectives to encourage more collaboration and have fewer individual goals.
8. Carefully consider what "reward" is – reward is not just money. Pay market-related salaries for skills and experience, but then think about other ways to reward employees such as time off, interaction with executives, project leads etc.

5.3. PREPARATION FOR THE PERFORMANCE APPRAISAL INTERVIEW

The following guidelines are designed to assist interviewers and interviewees.

5.3.1. Complete the preparation form

- Both the interviewer and interviewee need to complete the preparation form prior to the performance appraisal.

- Use this as a discussion document when completing the performance appraisal document in the interview.

- Ensure that enough information is on hand to be able to do an objective appraisal. If the information obtained through normal control of the employee is not sufficient, further information should be obtained at this stage.

- The interviewer and interviewee should study the definitions of elements of performance for clear explanations of what is meant by each factor.

An example of a performance appraisal preparation form is included below in Figure 5.2.

PREPARATION FORM
For general staff performance appraisal
PURPOSE
Both the interviewer and the interviewee need to complete the preparation form prior to the performance appraisal. Use this as a discussion document during the formal performance appraisal interview. Ensure that enough information is on hand to be able to do an objective appraisal. If the information obtained through normal control of the employee is not sufficient, further information should be obtained at this stage. The interviewer and interviewee should study the definitions of the behavioural factors for clear explanations of what is meant by each factor.
KEY RESPONSIBILITIES OR TASKS (KEY PERFORMANCE AREAS – KPAs): (The interviewer and the interviewee should agree on these up-front. These are normally taken from the job description and there could be up to six KPAs.)
BEHAVIOURAL FACTORS (Complete this section by describing your performance under each of these behavioural factors. Your performance should be evaluated bearing your KPAs in mind. Cite examples where necessary.) Volume of work _____

Quality and accuracy of work _____

Relationship with other staff members _____

Relationship with the company/equipment _____

Job knowledge and skills _____

Reliability and punctuality _____

Achievement of objectives _____

OBJECTIVES FOR NEXT REVIEW:

OBJECTIVE	STANDARD/MEASURE	TIME FRAME? DEADLINE DATE

DEVELOPMENT PLANS AND TRAINING REQUIREMENTS:

_____

_____

_____

_____

_____

_____

_____

_____

_____

_____

Figure 5.2: Example of a performance appraisal preparation form

5.3.2. Choose a suitable time and place for the interview

- It is important that sufficient time be allocated for the interview. Interruptions during the interview should be avoided.
- When the employee is informed of the interview, the manager should place the employee in the right frame of mind.
- The interview should take place in privacy.
- A proper appointment should be made well in advance for the interview so that both parties can prepare.
- Appraisal interviews should be planned well in advance of the target completion date to avoid a last-minute rush.

5.3.3. Decide how the interview should be approached

It is important to note that an employee's attitude in respect of the performance appraisal depends to a great degree on the manager's attitude. Managers should understand that employees must be convinced of their genuine effort and resolve to make the system work and to honour commitments made during the performance appraisal session.

5.4. THE PERFORMANCE APPRAISAL INTERVIEW

The following guidelines should be followed when conducting the performance appraisal interview:

5.4.1. Create a friendly atmosphere

Managers should not only establish a friendly atmosphere at the beginning of the interview, but should also concentrate on putting the employee at ease throughout the interview. Under no circumstances should managers use their position to manipulate or overpower the employee.

5.4.2. Ensure that the employee understands the purpose of the interview

The manager could explain the objective of the interview as follows:

> "The objective of this interview is to discuss your performance during the past year and to decide if you have performed to the requirements for the job during this period. If you have not met the requirements, what can we do to improve your performance?"

Employees should understand the following:

- In order to progress, clear plans have to be made jointly with their managers in respect of their own improvement and training.
- Development depends on the assessment of potential, and (although not always pleasant) progress will be impaired if weaknesses are not identified.

- Their own needs and objectives will be appraised in conjunction with those of the organisation.
- Monitoring of progress will take place through the total system of performance appraisal.
- Their salary increases will be linked to the result of the performance appraisal.
- Juniors and beginners can expect to receive ratings that imply that further development is required because special effort on their part will be required in order to meet the job requirements.
- A high rating may still go together with constructive suggestions in respect of aspects that can be improved.
- They have the right to question or challenge their appraisal results through the appropriate channels, in this case, the HR department. Formal grievance procedures may be followed if the employee feels the need to go this route once discussions with his or her manager and a HR representative have taken place.

5.4.3. Complete the performance appraisal form together

The performance appraisal form should now be completed together, using the preparation forms as a basis for discussion. Two examples of performance appraisal forms are provided below in Figures 5.3 and 5.4. The first form can be used for general staff, while the second form is designed for managers. The advantage of these two standardised forms with common dimensions for all general staff jobs and all managerial jobs is ease of use, consistency, and getting up to speed quickly. A step-by-step guide on how to complete these forms follows.

PERFORMANCE APPRAISAL FORM
GENERAL
PURPOSE
To provide the employee and management with a comprehensive evaluation of the employee's current performance and potential, in order to
<table><tr><td>- improve performance on the present job</td><td>- strengthen the manager–employee relationship</td></tr><tr><td>- provide for the development of the employee</td><td>- provide management with current data for use in its</td></tr><tr><td>- reward high performance</td><td>organisation planning efforts</td></tr></table>
PROCEDURE
1. The performance appraisal form is to be completed by the employee's immediate supervisor.
2. Give much thought and careful consideration to your appraisal. Be objective and do not allow personal feelings to influence your evaluation.
3. Check the rating that most adequately describes the employee's performance.
4. Forward the numerical rating to the score column in the shaded section.
5. When completed, this form will be reviewed with the next-higher level of management before being discussed with the employee being rated.
6. Conduct a private conference with the employee. Stress outstanding abilities, explain necessary improvements, and allow the employee time to make comments.

7. Agree and finalise ratings with the employee in the columns that are not shaded.

8. When the discussion is finished, each employee will sign, signifying that he or she has seen the report and has been counselled. Should the employee feel that the report is unfair, a meeting between the supervisor and the next level of management may be requested.

9. The completed form should be forwarded through department management to the HR Department.

Name:_____	Job title: _____
Department/branch: _____	Starting date with company: _____
Date appointed to this position: _____	Job grade: _____
Period of appraisal : _____ to _____	Today's date: _____
Supervisor's name:_____	Supervisor's job: _____
Title:_____	

KEY RESPONSIBILITIES OR TASKS (KEY PERFORMANCE AREAS [KPAs] – weighted in order of priority):

Job-specific

1. _____

1. _____

1. _____

1. _____

1. _____

1. _____

Generic

1. _____

1. _____

1. _____

PERFORMANCE RATING SCALE:

5. FAR EXCEEDS REQUIREMENTS	Incumbent has far exceeded requirements.
4. EXCEEDS REQUIREMENTS	Incumbent has exceeded requirements.
3. MEETS REQUIREMENTS	Incumbent has met requirements.
2. MEETS SOME REQUIREMENTS	Incumbent has not met requirements in some key areas. Some improvement necessary.
1. DOES NOT MEET THE REQUIREMENTS	Incumbent is not meeting requirements in most key areas. Much improvement necessary.

WORK OBJECTIVES	PERFORMANCE RATING AS MEASURED AGAINST KEY REPONSIBILITIES				
	5	4	3	2	1
1. VOLUME OF WORK (Output, amount of work, ability to do more in times of crisis, maintaining high work rate/speed.)					
2. QUALITY AND ACCURACY (Maintaining a high quality of work, accurate in completing tasks.)					
3. RELATIONSHIP WITH OTHER STAFF MEMBERS (Maintaining harmonious relations, constructive and beneficial or motivating influence on others.)					
4. RELATIONSHIP WITH THE COMPANY/EQUIPMENT (Proper application of systems, adherence to rules, caring and maintaining property and safeguarding interests.)					
5. RELIABILITY AND PUNCTUALITY (Can one depend on this employee, is he/she timeous, does he/she stick to the schedule/time limits?)					
6. COMPETENCIES AND ATTRIBUTES – JOB KNOWLEDGE AND SKILLS (Refers to proven mastery of the finer points, and identifying areas of improvement.)					
7. ACHIEVEMENT OF OBJECTIVES (To what extent were the objectives achieved as set in the previous appraisal or on starting in this post?)					

TOTAL SCORE (out of 35)

OTHER KEY PERFORMANCE INDICATORS NOT LISTED ABOVE:

_____

_____

_____

EMPLOYEE RESPONSE AND COMMENTS:

_____

_____

_____

OBJECTIVES FOR NEXT REVIEW

EMPLOYEE (Write down objectives and improvement targets for the next performance appraisal. Set a standard or measure.)

OBECTIVE/ IMPROVEMENT TARGET	STANDARD/MEASURE	TIME FRAME/ DEADLINE DATE

SUPERVISOR (What objectives or improvement targets would you like to set for the employee?)

OBECTIVE/ IMPROVEMENT TARGET	STANDARD/MEASURE	TIME FRAME/ DEADLINE DATE

DEVELOPMENT PLANS AND TRAINING REQUIREMENTS

Can be identified from areas where high and low ratings were awarded above.

STRENGTHS/SPECIAL SKILLS: _____

_____

_____

_____

_____

AREAS FOR DEVELOPMENT; KNOWLEDGE/SKILLS GAPS (PRIORITISE THESE IN ORDER FOR THEM TO BE INCLUDED IN THE WORKPLACE SKILLS PLAN): _____

_____

_____

_____

_____

_____

AREAS REQUIRING ATTENTION: _____

_____

_____

_____

_____

DEVELOPMENT PLANS: _____

_____

_____

_____

_____

RECOMMENDATIONS, SPECIFIC ACTIONS, TRAINING REQUIREMENTS: _____

_____

_____

_____

_____

Employee's signature:_____ Date:_____

Supervisor's signature:_____ Date: _____

Reviewer's signature:_____Date: _____

Figure 5.3: Example of a performance appraisal form for general staff

PERFORMANCE APPRAISAL FORM

MANAGEMENT

PURPOSE

To provide the employee and management with a comprehensive evaluation of the manager's current performance and potential, in order to

- improve performance on the present job
- strengthen the manager–employee relationship
- provide for the development of the employee
- provide management with current data for use in its organisation planning efforts
- reward high performance

PROCEDURE

1. The performance appraisal form is to be completed by the employee's immediate supervisor.

2. Give much thought and careful consideration to your appraisal. Be objective and do not allow personal feelings to influence your evaluation.

3. Check the rating that most adequately describes the employee's performance.

4. Forward the numerical rating to the score column in the shaded section.

5. When completed, this form will be reviewed with the next-higher level of management before being discussed with the employee being rated.

6. Conduct a private conference with the employee. Stress outstanding abilities, explain necessary improvements, and allow the employee time to make comments.

7. Agree and finalise ratings with the employee in the columns that are not shaded.

8. When the discussion is finished, each employee will sign, signifying that he/she has seen the report and has been counselled. Should the employee feel that the report is unfair, a meeting between the supervisor and the next level of management may be requested.

9. The completed form should be forwarded through department management to the HR Department.

Name:_____   Job title: _____

Department/branch: _____   Starting date with company: _____

Date appointed to this position: _____   Job grade: _____

Period of appraisal: _____ to _____   Today's date: _____

Supervisor's name:_____   Supervisor's job: _____

Title:_____

KEY RESPONSIBILITIES OR TASKS (KEY PERFORMANCE AREAS [KPAs] – weighted in order of priority):

Job-specific

1. _____

2. _____

3. _____

4. _____

5. _____

6. _____

Generic

7. _____

8. _____

9. _____

PERFORMANCE RATING SCALE:

5. FAR EXCEEDS REQUIREMENTS — Incumbent has far exceeded requirements.

4. EXCEEDS REQUIREMENTS — Incumbent has exceeded requirements.

3. MEETS REQUIREMENTS — Incumbent has met requirements.

2. MEETS SOME REQUIREMENTS — Incumbent has not met requirements in some key areas. Some improvement necessary.

1. DOES NOT MEET THE REQUIREMENTS — Incumbent is not meeting requirements in most key areas. Much improvement necessary.

WORK OBJECTIVES	PERFORMANCE RATING AS MEASURED AGAINST KEY REPONSIBILITIES				
	5	4	3	2	1
1. FINANCE MANAGEMENT (Are budgets set accurately and kept to, are finances used optimally, are expenses reduced, is he/she fostering conservation attitudes amongst employees?)					
2. GOALS AND PRODUCTIVITY (Clarification of goals and encouragement given to employees. Maintenance of high standards, and effectiveness of department.)					
3. WORK ORGANISATION (Was work organised methodically and were correct communication channels established? To what extent were conflicting priorities managed? Was coordinated teamwork achieved?)					

4. LEADING AND CONTROLLING (The ability to create trust and respect, achieve teamwork, and assure employees of direction and control.)					
5. PLANNING (Refers to the ability to accomplish tasks timeously, and the preparation of short- and long-term plans. Recognition of problems and contingency planning.)					
6. KNOWLEDGE (Refers to the ability to apply correct principles and techniques, accurate interpretation of user requirements, and the extent of keeping abreast of developments.)					
7. APPRAISAL AND DEVELOPMENT OF SUBORIDINATES (The ability to train and develop subordinates, provide feedback on performance, and the successful mentoring and coaching of subordinates.)					
8. PROBLEM SOLVING AND DECISION MAKING (Refers to the ability to use given information to solve problems and make decisions. Timeous decisions under pressure and extent to which problems are solved before handing over to seniors.)					
9. LIVING ORGANISATIONAL IDEALS (Refers to the extent to which there has been an alignment to the culture and ideals that the organisation values.)					
10. ACHIEVEMENT OF OBJECTIVES (To what extent were the objectives achieved as set in the previous appraisal or on starting in this post?)					

TOTAL SCORE (out of 50)

OTHER KEY PERFORMANCE INDICATORS NOT LISTED ABOVE:

_____

_____

_____

_____

EMPLOYEE RESPONSE AND COMMENTS:

_____

_____

_____

_____

81

Key performance area	Outputs	Key performance indicators
Job-specific		
Major outputs specific to the position	Achievable outcomes	Measurements for KPAs – should be tangible
Generic		
Major generic outputs for the individual in the organisation		

Figure 5.4: Example of a managerial performance appraisal form

The performance appraisal forms should be completed as follows:

• Complete the section headed "Personal details".

• Agree on, and complete, the section headed "Key performance areas (KPAs)". These KPAs form the major components of the employee's job. They are referred to in the job profile.

• Complete the rating of **each** KPA against the elements of performance, and any additional key performance indicators using the rating scale of 1–5 (see next section for a description of these). Please note that, for the factor "Achievement of objectives", we are rating the objectives that were set for the year that has just passed.

• Agree on, and complete, the section "**Objectives for next review**". These objectives need to have a standard or measure so that one can tell without much doubt whether the objective was met. For example, it is difficult to measure the objective, "To improve my typing". It is better to state the objective as, "To improve my typing, **and** the measure", which could be from 30 to 40 words per minute with 95 per cent accuracy. In this way, we can all see whether or not the objective was met.

• The discussion must now turn to the future. Complete the section headed "Development plans and training requirements". This aspect will be reasonably dealt with if the following questions receive clear and favourable answers:

  o What has to be improved?
  o What specific objectives are being set (target figures, error rates, proficiency levels, etc.)?
  o What methods for achieving these results are to be adopted?
  o How can procedures previously tried without success be modified?
  o What specific actions can be taken to improve performance, eg formal training courses, job rotation, informal training through specific discussions, opportunities to observe or participate in new functions?
  o What higher-level opportunities may be available to the employee, and what ability and performance standards are required before these opportunities will be considered?
  o What personal needs, preferences or dislikes on the part of the employee are to be considered in planning his/her development?
  o Has the employee been "steam-rollered" in the discussion so that important points from his/her side are made only afterwards to colleagues in a destructive or negative way?

- This discussion conducted successfully leads to a mutually-agreed-upon plan for the employee following the period until the next formal assessment.
- Sign and date the performance appraisal form. The completed form should be sent to the HR Department **after** it has been signed by the reviewer (next level of management). Remember to make copies of the forms for your own records.

5.5. PRACTICAL GUIDELINES TO BE USED IN THE APPROACH TO THE INTERVIEW

- Use the "sandwich" technique. Mention areas in the employee's work that need improvement, between positive aspects.
- Emphasise the reason for the appraisal.
- Give the employee enough opportunity to voice his/her opinion about the appraisal, for this might explain the reason for performance that does not meet the requirements.
- Never get aggressive during an interview, irrespective of what an employee says. STAY CALM.
- Provide enough time for the employee to accept the appraisal – acceptance of criticism does not always come immediately.
- Do not try to convince the employee of anything while he/she is aggressive.
- Play the ball, not the person.
- If remarks in respect of personality or behaviour are made, they should never be vague – say exactly what is meant and substantiate with examples.
- Show interest in the employee's work-related problems.
- Provide positive criticism and suggestions. If an area for improvement is discussed, offer a possible solution or an improvement of the method.
- Ensure that the employee understands that the appraisal of his/her performance can change the next time round, but that the onus to improve is upon him/her.
- Be willing to listen and discuss, but be very firm.
- Ensure that the employee understands what is expected of him/her.
- Do not be afraid to praise good performance, as this can improve the employee's work satisfaction, and positively influence attitudes.
- End the interview with a summary of strengths and areas for improvement, and summarise the plan of action.
- The emphasis should be on comparing an employee against the requirements set for the position/grade, not against the performance of other employees. Where a number of employees perform the same functions under similar circumstances, comparisons can be made to increase the objectivity of the ratings. Managers should give some consideration to the tightening of requirements for all jobs so that the requirements set at a given level or job grade make comparable demands on employees.
- When an employee has been in the organisation or work team for too short a period for a proper assessment of his/her performance to be obtained, a suitable postponement of the event will ensure that an unsubstantiated, unfair and ultimately destructive result is avoided.

5.5.1. Pitfalls that should be avoided in evaluating performance

The Halo Effect

- Performance in previous years should not affect the present evaluation. The performance being evaluated is only for the period noted on the first page of the form.
- Avoid the tendency to praise likeable/unlikeable employees higher/lower than deserved.
- A single, outstanding task should not influence the whole performance; look at the employee's performance as a whole.
- Do not disregard mistakes that you yourself may have made.
- Be objective.
- Do not appraise a person for good potential; appraise for what has actually been done.

Perfectionism/nonperfectionism

- The manager expects too much from employees and evaluates too low, or the supervisor's standards are too low and he/she appraises too high. Avoid bunching all employees in only part of the scale.

External factors

- Ensure that problems outside the workplace do not affect the rating you give to employees. Always remember to appraise employees objectively.

5.6. ASPECTS OR DIMENSIONS OF WORK TO BE RATED AND COMMENTED UPON

A good employee may have specific developmental needs that can be addressed by identifying them, by proper planning, and by discussing solutions with the individual. A poor performer can be more easily motivated if strengths are accurately assessed and he or she understands that there is no managerial prejudice. The mistake of uncritically giving an employee identical ratings for all performance aspects to save time should be avoided.

The following are commonly used aspects or dimensions of work to be rated and commented upon. Of course, these should be replaced with dimensions that may be more appropriate for your organisation.

5.6.1. The general appraisal form

Volume of work (output, amount of work)

Aspects to consider under volume include the following:

- the ability to do more when under pressure
- the ability to maintain a high work rate/speed
- the ability to complete tasks and not only to "have a lot of work"

Remember that the rating of accuracy is a separate item and should only be considered if everything (or most things) is done incorrectly at high speed by the employee. When volume is commented upon for employee development purposes, it should be related to output and deadlines, correct methods, sequence of tasks, planning of time spent, et cetera, in order to assist the employee in increasing his or her output.

Quality and accuracy

While many jobs have specified error rates, supervisors should ensure that they know how well their subordinates fare on this aspect, irrespective of whether or not formal records are kept as a normal function. Remember that the isolated incident should not be overemphasised in the rating. The regular omission of smaller points in a total process, the extent to which an error could/should have been foreseen, the care with which the correct methods are used, and the degree of checking should impact the evaluation of this dimension.

Suggestions should also be made in respect of specific training needs, self-improvement steps and targets to be set for the employee's next assessment.

Relationships with other staff members

Maintaining harmonious relations, as well as preventing these relations from becoming a time-wasting or interference factor in productivity, should be considered as a general tendency in the employee's behaviour over the time period. The highly positive assessment will also be related to a constructive, beneficial or motivating influence on others and not only to a neutral one of "getting on" with co-workers.

Relationship with the organisation

Acceptance of authority, adherence to rules, willingness to cooperate, proper application of systems, and care in maintaining property and safeguarding assets are a number of the disciplinary aspects that, in some form, apply to every job in the organisation. While the rater should comment on specific issues relevant to the job of the employee concerned, this aspect should be summarised in the overall judgement in order to arrive at a rating decision.

Reliability and punctuality

The employee should meet deadlines as set out in the job description at a consistently high level. The company should be able to depend on the employee in respect of job performance and reliability in assuming and carrying out the commitments and obligations of his or her position.

Competencies and attributes – job knowledge and skill

A high rating should be reserved for top-class performance in the most important components of the job, together with proven mastery of the finer points, and knowledge of methods, techniques and skills in the employee's functional field.

Achievement of objectives

This relates to the extent to which the employee achieved the objectives as set out in the previous appraisal or on starting in the post.

5.6.2. The management appraisal form

The following guidelines and questions should assist raters in the completion of the management appraisal. These areas of competence may refer to aspects of a manager's key performance areas (KPAs).

Finance management

The criteria are as follows:

- The accuracy of budget setting and whether budgets were met
- The utilisation of finances and resources to maximise opportunities
- The establishment of cost controls
- The identification of opportunities to reduce expenses
- The fostering of cost and conservation attitudes amongst employees

Goals and productivity

The criteria are as follows:

- The way in which a manager clarifies the organisation's goals for employees, and the encouragement given
- The efficiency and effectiveness of the division or department
- The maintenance of high performance standards in line with organisational objectives
- The accomplishment of the position's objectives whilst maintaining quality

Work organisation

The criteria are as follows:

- The methodical organisation of own and employees' work
- The clarity of work relationships and channels of communication
- The handling of conflicting priorities or demands, and appropriate assignment of resources
- Effective time management
- Achievement of coordinated teamwork

Leading and controlling

The criteria are as follows:

- The cooperation and teamwork in the division/department
- The motivation of employees, and the building of *esprit de corps*, trust and respect
- The adaptation of management style to different people and situations
- Regular follow-up of implementation of action plans
- The assurance of direction and control

Planning

The criteria are as follows:

- The selection of the best route to accomplish tasks timeously and with minimum difficulty
- The preparation of short- and long-term plans, and setting priorities in attaining them
- The recognition of possible problems in advance and preparation of contingency plans
- The avoidance of having to redo or take over subordinates' work

Knowledge

The criteria are as follows:

- The application of correct principles and techniques to tasks
- The accurate interpretation of user requirements
- The extent of guidance required by the manager
- The extent to which the manager keeps abreast of developments in his/her field

Appraisal and development of subordinates

The criteria are as follows:

- The training and development of subordinates to their maximum potential
- The negotiation of challenging work objectives and provision of feedback on performance
- The establishment of development plans
- Successful coaching and counselling of subordinates

Problem solving and decision making

The criteria are as follows:

- The integration and use of all available information to solve problems and make decisions
- The formation of independent opinions and thorough objective analysis of problems
- The extent to which problems are solved before handing over to seniors
- Timeous decisions even under pressure
- The skilfulness in solving problems inherent in work
- The analytical competence of the manager

Living the organisation ideals

The criterion is as follows:

- Aligning to the organisational culture.

Achievement of objectives

The criterion is as follows:

- The extent to which the objectives, as set out in the previous performance appraisal, were achieved.

NOTE: There may be circumstances where not all criteria are applicable to the person being rated. In this case, leave out the criteria that do not apply. The formula to use is as follows:

$$\frac{\text{Actual score}}{\text{Actual possible total}} \times \text{Total possible (all criteria)}$$

For example, if an employee was appraised on the managerial appraisal form and the score obtained for 8 criteria was 28, the formula would be applied as follows:

$$\frac{28}{40} \times 50 = 35$$

Thirty-five would be the amount captured as the performance appraisal score.

5.7. THE PERFORMANCE RATING SCALE AND REWARD IMPLICATION

The elements of performance are rated, for example, on a five-point rating scale, and Figure 5.5. summarises the features of the points scale. It is important to note that "requirements" refers to the requirements as set out and recognised by the organisation. It is the organisation's expectations of what is needed and required. This is an example of a five-point rating scale. There are numerous other rating scales that can be used. These are elaborated on in the following chapter (chapter 7 – Performance appraisal rating scales).

Performance rating scale		
Scale point	**Performance description**	**Reward implication**
5	Far exceeds requirements	Deserving of a special reward or merit increase
4	Exceeds requirements	Should receive an above-average increase
3	Meets requirements	Deserving of the percentage increment top management sets for the company in general
2	Meets some requirements	Should receive a restricted increase, lower than the average increase
1	Does not meet requirements	An increase should not be given or a very small one should be given

Figure 5.5: The performance rating scale and reward implications

It could be very costly to the organisation if nearly all employees scored a 5. For this to be the case, there would probably be an unusual circumstance surrounding it. It would be more usual, however, for the scores to be normally distributed among the five-point scales. (This serves only as a **guideline** to be used by management in respect of how many people should fall into each category.) Top management may allow deviations from this in line with exceptional or unusual circumstances, especially if a specific department has done particularly well.

Figure 5.6. serves as a **guideline** as to what the desired distribution should be for the entire organisation. (This may or may not be the case for each department.)

Description	Scale score range		Desired distribution
	General	Managerial	
Far exceeds (5)	32-35	46-50	Less than 10%
Exceeds (4)	27-31	39-45	Around 20%
Meets requirements (3)	19-26	22-38	Around 40%
Meets some (2)	13-18	15-21	Around 20%
Does not meet (1)	8-12	10-14	Less than 10%

Figure 5.6: Guideline for total performance rating distributions

NOTE: It cannot be overstressed that this is merely management information, and is to be used as a guideline for managing hard and soft raters.

5.8. PROBLEMS WITH THE TRADITIONAL APPROACH TO PERFORMANCE APPRAISAL

There are numerous challenges regarding the traditional approach to performance appraisal. Some of these are tabulated in Figure 5.7. below.

Problem	Implication
Focuses on results rather than behaviour	Organisations often place inordinate emphasis on production numbers when making remuneration and promotional decisions and ignore the behaviours that lead to end results.
Addresses vast and complex information	Rather than focus on issues of strategic value, many performance management systems inundate employees with detailed operational feedback; developmental information should focus on areas that significantly influence overall business goals.
Lack of balance between development and appraisal	Performance management systems provide evaluation, appraisal and developmental data; organisations often fail to emphasise developmental aspects, creating programmes that are purely retrospective in nature and promote a negative atmosphere.
Lack of ownership among senior and line management	HR often assumes responsibility for performance management systems owing to its relationship with human assets; however, line management should internalise systems as management processes and utilise HR as internal consultants.

Figure 5.7: Problems with the traditional approach to performance appraisal

5.9. EMPLOYEE PERFORMANCE APPRAISAL CHECK LIST

One of the keys to success in performance appraisal is adequate preparation. The following check list is designed as a guide to preparing, conducting and following through on employee performance appraisal discussions.

1.   **PERSONAL PREPARATION**

☐ I have reviewed mutually understood expectations with respect to job duties, projects, objectives, and any other predetermined performance factors pertinent to this appraisal discussion.

☐ I have observed job performance measured against mutually understood expectations. In so doing, I have done my best to avoid such pitfalls as the following:

_____   Bias/prejudice

_____   The vagaries of memory

_____   Overattention to some aspects of the job at the expense of others

_____   Being overly influenced by my own experience

_____   Trait appraisal rather than performance measurement

☐ I have reviewed the employee's background including, for example:

_____   Skills

_____   Work experience

_____   Training

☐ I have determined the employee's performance and strengths, and areas in need of improvement, and in so doing have done the following:

_____   Accumulated specific, unbiased documentation that can be used to help communicate my position

_____   Limited myself to those critical points that are the most important

_____   Prepared a possible development plan in case the employee needs assistance in coming up with a suitable plan

_____   Identified prioritised skills needs for use in the annual Workplace Skills Plan

☐ I have identified areas to be concentrated on in setting objectives and standards for the next appraisal period.

☐ I have given the employee advance notice of when the discussion will be held so that he/she can prepare.

☐ I have set aside an adequate block of uninterrupted time to permit a full and complete discussion.

2. CONDUCTING THE APPRAISAL DISCUSSION

☐ I plan to begin the discussion by creating a sincere, but open and friendly atmosphere. This includes the following:

_____ Reviewing the purpose of the discussion

_____ Making it clear that it is a joint discussion for the purpose of mutual problem solving and goal setting

_____ Striving to put the employee at ease

☐ In the body of the discussion, I intend to keep the focus on job performance and related factors. This includes the following:

_____ Discussing job requirements – employee strengths, accomplishments, and improvement needs, and evaluating results of performance against objectives set during previous review discussions

_____ Being prepared to cite observations for each point I want to discuss

_____ Encouraging the employee to appraise his/her own performance

_____ Using open, reflective and directive questions to promote thought, understanding and problem solving

☐ I will encourage the employee to outline his/her personal plans for self-development before suggesting ideas of my own. In the process, I will do the following:

_____ Try to get the employee to set personal growth and improvement targets

_____ Strive to reach agreement on appropriate development plans which detail what the employee intends to do, on a timetable, and on support I am prepared to give

☐ I am prepared to discuss work assignments, projects and objectives for the next appraisal period and will ask the employee to come prepared with suggestions.

3. CLOSING THE DISCUSSION

☐ I will be prepared to make notes during the discussion for the purpose of summarising agreements and follow-up. In closing, I will do the following:

_____ Summarise what has been discussed

_____ Show enthusiasm for plans that have been made

_____ Give the employee an opportunity to make additional suggestions

_____ End on a positive, friendly, harmonious note

4. **POSTAPPRAISAL FOLLOW-UP**

☐ As soon as the discussion is over, I will record the plans made, the points requiring follow-up, the commitments I made, and I will provide a copy for the employee.

☐ I will also evaluate how I handled the discussion by considering the following:

_____ What I did well

_____ What I could have done better

_____ What I learnt about the employee and his/her job

_____ What I learnt about myself and my job

Figure 5.8: Employee performance appraisal check list

5.10. CONCLUSION

The comprehensive performance appraisal system can, if applied correctly, ensure that fairness, continuity in development planning, and management involvement in staff advancement are maintained. It is necessary to remember the following important points:

- Rate objectively.
- Diagnose, and comment effectively on, employee strengths and areas for improvement.
- Listen effectively to establish the employee's own perceptions and convictions regarding the work, the way he/she is treated, career needs and aspirations, and special areas of concern.
- Interview effectively when giving feedback and when planning for the following period of work.

Performance appraisal training is the responsibility of the HR Department. Assistance in improving existing procedures to include and integrate all the related aspects of the total system should be made available. The emphasis in this system must be on flexible adjustment to local circumstances, and acceptance by, and involvement of, all staff, rather than on rigid uniformity.

5.11. BIBLIOGRAPHY

Chandler, M.T. 2016. *How performance management is killing performance – and what to do about it.* Berrett-Koehler.

Endnotes

55. Chandler, 2016.

6 PERFORMANCE APPRAISAL RATING SCALES

6.1. INTRODUCTION

Often, human resource (HR) specialists are asked to develop a performance rating scale that will be "best practice". There are many organisations that change their performance rating system every few years, as it is seen as "the silver bullet" that will heal all ailments that are experienced with the performance management process. As long as performance management is used in organisations, performance evaluations will be here to stay. A well-written, clearly defined performance rating scale can simplify performance evaluations, which are a focal point in the performance management process of identifying key performance and development issues, and, if done well, will result in increased employee engagement and productivity.

This chapter will focus on the most prevalent rating scales used in the performance review process.

Deloitte – "Why ratings breed disappointment"

Deloitte is one of a number of large multi-nationals looking to "reboot" the performance management process. Perhaps their most controversial change has been to do away with ratings and distribution targets.

Many people would balk at the idea of doing away with ratings – they are easy and you can plot people on a performance scale, creating a good visual overview of how the individual and the team is performing. This ease of use, however, comes at a cost. In addition to the difficulty in trying to make performance ratings as objective as possible, they are pretty much disliked by everyone who has to implement them!

Deloitte's view is that:

- Ratings and distribution targets make the assumption that performance is one dimensional – reducing performance to a target negates the complexity of tasks and does not reflect the performance objectively or even describe what went into the performance.

- Forced ranking assumes that performance is evenly distributed – it is not realistic to think 10% of the company are low performers, 10% are high performers and the rest somewhere in the middle. Forced distribution is demotivating for the majority of high performers as their ability to be ranked near the top is not dependent on their performance alone.

- Rater bias impacts performance ratings – ratings are prone to the 'recency' effect (where only the most recent behaviour is remembered) and ratings are heavily dependent on the subjective input of the rater.

- Ratings breed competition not collaboration.

Overall, Deloitte views ratings as demotivating and unnecessary. They now prefer the richness of frequent feedback, evidence, and forward-looking reviews (Deloitte, 2015).

The performance rating scales described in this chapter all have a place when used appropriately. While some companies like Deloitte may have had success in eliminating ratings, performance ratings are definitely still a useful tool for the majority of companies and will continue to be used in the future.

6.2. REVIEWING PERFORMANCE

The main purpose of a performance rating scale is to assist managers in formalising their judgement of an employee's performance over a certain period of time. The performance judgement is then categorised on a scale which informs performance incentives, and often annual increases, and is also used for record-keeping purposes relating to the employee's performance over a period of time. According to Armstrong[56], there are four arguments for rating employees' performance:

- Ratings recognise the fact that managers form an overall view of the performance of people reporting to them. They express this view in terms of a rating, using an accepted framework. By doing this, managers can be held accountable to justify the rating given to an employee in terms of his or her performance.

- Ratings are useful to sum up performance assessment, and, particularly, in identifying exceptional and reliable performers, and underperformers.

- Ratings are required as a means to distribute performance-based incentives and increases.

- By giving a rating on past performance, a clear message is given to an employee on how he or she is performing, and what he or she needs to do to improve on his or her performance.

The frequency of performance reviews required to be done in organisations varies. In a study undertaken by the Corporate Leadership Council (CLC), it was found that 51 per cent of organisations conduct formal performance reviews once per financial year, while 41 per cent of organisations require performance reviews to be conducted at least twice per year. It was further reported that, of the organisations conducting performance reviews in the middle of a year, these are done mostly informally.[57]

Over a number of years, a variety of different performance appraisal methods have been developed, such as personnel comparison systems, critical-incident techniques, behaviourally anchored rating scales, mixed-standard scales and multiple-step scales. For purposes of this chapter, however, the main differentiators of the rating scales mostly used are that they are numeric, alphabetic, narrative or graphic. Organisations using balanced scorecards mostly assess performance in percentage terms, but, often, these percentages are related back to a numeric score for purposes of increase and incentive distribution.

6.3. COMMONLY USED RATING SCALES

A variety of disparate rating scales occur in practice. Fifty-one per cent of organisations use either numeric or qualitative scales. It is also becoming common practice to use a combination of both numeric rating scales and narrative descriptions in the performance review process. A multiple-step scale provides for ratings on any of several rating categories, which are defined in terms of numbers, adjectives or brief descriptors. Albeit that organisations find the five-point rating scale problematic owing to issues with central tendency (where most ratings are clustered around the middle of a five-point rating scale), it is apparent that this is still the most commonly used scale. There is no scientific evidence that clearly indicates that one scale is superior to another, but the greater the number of levels, the more is being asked of managers in terms of discriminatory judgement. The following are examples of performance rating scales most commonly used in organisations.

6.3.1. Numeric scales

Two-point scales

These scales are the least commonly used, and mostly so in organisations that encourage binary thinking, that is, you either achieve or you don't. Typically, employees who did not achieve their objectives are required to leave if they don't improve their performance over a reasonable period of time.

Three-point scales

Three-point scales are typically associated with a target distribution curve, and this is considered a very simple approach. Managers are mostly required to identify top- and low-performers.

The CLC[58] provides the following scale labels that are frequently used in a three-point scale:

1*	2	3
←		→
Exceptional	Effective	Improvement required
Exceeds expectations	Meets expectations	Does not meet expectations
Top	Core	Low
Exceptional performer	Full performer	Developer
Walking on water	Swimming	Sinking

*Rating 1 is the highest rating, followed by lower ratings.

By using this scale, outstanding performers are recognised, but then to such an extent that the truly exceptional performers are not singled out. On the other hand, whilst the underperformers can be very clearly identified, there is not sufficient differentiation between employees just not making the grade and those who missed all their objectives. It is therefore mostly found that a three-point scale does not provide sufficient differentiation in performance, particularly for organisations that use performance as a means to differentiate in increases and incentives. This means that there is a greater reliance on managerial judgement with these kinds of remuneration decisions, which require a culture of trust and flexibility to succeed. For this reason, managers often enquire whether they can add a "plus" or a "minus" or decimals to the numeric scale to provide them with a sense of differentiation. Owing to the lack of granularity in performance definition, more guidelines therefore need to be provided for line managers to ensure consistent and fair performance assessments.

Four-point scales

Four- and six-point scales are mainly used in organisations that want managers to apply greater differentiation in the performance evaluation process and so avoid central tendency. This scale has also been used with great success in organisations that have been working hard on improving their organisational climate, where the descriptors are focused on providing positive reinforcement. The four-point scale is becoming more popular with organisations, as there is no central-tendency problem, and it is fairly simple to link with performance-based remuneration schemes.

The CLC[59] provides the following scale labels that are frequently used in a four-point scale:

1*	2	3	4
←			→
Outstanding	Above expectations	Meets expectations	Below expectations
Outstanding	Exceeds expectations	Meets expectations	Needs improvement
Outstanding performance	Strong performance	Good performance	Inconsistent performance
Significantly exceeding	Exceeding	Performing	Developing
Mastery	High	Solid	Novice
Highly effective	Effective	Developing	Basic

*Rating 1 is the highest rating, followed by lower ratings.

Five-point scales

Five-point rating scales are the most frequently used performance rating scales, and the most common is the Likert-type scale. This scale is used to assess performance around a central point, which is widely interpreted by employers as "acceptable" performance. The primary concern with the five-point scale is that the central point is considered by employees as "average performance" as opposed to being at the intended level where all objectives have been met. As employees generally do not want to be perceived as average performers, the final rating conversation is often quite challenging, with employees arguing that their performance rating should be higher than the midpoint, being a "3".

The CLC[60] provides the following scale labels that are frequently used in a five-point scale:

1*	2	3	4	5
←				→
Outstanding	Excellent	Fully effective	Needs improvement	Unacceptable
Consistently exceeds expectations	Sometimes exceeds expectations	Consistently meets expectations	Sometimes meets expectations	Does not meet expectations
Exemplary	Strong performance	Proficient	Needs development	Must be improved
Among the best	Highly effective	Fully productive	Developing	Needs improvement
Stellar	Outstanding	Good, solid performance	Met some	Did not meet

*Rating 1 is the highest rating, followed by lower ratings.

One of the advantages of a five-point rating scale is that it provides two opportunities for superior performance (likewise, two opportunities for less effective performance). Managers making the final assessment can, in addition to the individual's performance against the agreed objectives, also take into consideration the relative complexity of the role as well as the environment within which the employee operates in order to arrive at a fair, balanced performance rating.

Six-point scales

Albeit less popular, six-point rating scales can be useful in organisations where performance can be differentiated in a more granulated manner than would, for example, be required in a four-point rating scale.

Armstrong and Murlis and the CLC[61] provide examples of labels that can be used in this type of scale:

1*	2	3	4	5	6
←					→
A	B	C+	C	C-	D
Exceptional performance	Excellent performance	Well-balanced performance	Reasonable performance	Barely effective performance	Unacceptable performance
Individual performance targets consistently exceed requirements	Individual performance targets generally exceed requirements on most occasions	Individual performance targets achieved, meeting requirements on all occasions	Individual performance targets achieved, exceeding requirements on a few occasions	Individual performance targets generally achieved, with a few occasions of partially meeting requirements	Individual performance does not meet requirements
Outstanding	Excellent	Met all targets	Met most targets	Met some targets	Did not meet targets
Top performer	Outstanding performer	Highly successful performer	Successful performer	Development performer	Needs improvement

*Rating 1 is the highest rating, followed by lower ratings.

Organisations using six-point rating scales need to ensure that their line managers spend adequate time with employees drawing up detailed performance scorecards, with very specific measures linked to the six ratings to ensure the objective assessment of performance. Adequate training for line managers in advance becomes more imperative the more detailed the rating scale is.

Also, as a wider range of labels is used, the descriptors used in qualifying the different ratings are clear and precise. In addition, the meaning behind the central rating must be positioned positively to ensure that no negative perceptions are created around one's performance being "average".

Seven- and eight-point rating scales

As seven- and eight-point rating scales require much more detailed descriptors, and a lot more judgement and involvement on the part of managers, they are less popular among organisations. Research has found that these types of rating scales are much more accurate if they include the use of behavioural anchors that define what good and poor performance look like in terms of specifically observable and well-defined behaviours – by doing this, and by providing training for line managers, this type of scale could significantly increase the quality of feedback given to employees regarding their performance.

When seven- and eight-point scales are used, the start and end points on the scale (1 and 7/8) should be used as the two absolute extremes. If 1 on the scale represents exemplary performance, 7/8 will represent unacceptable, poor performance which warrants immediate action in terms of performance-improvement plans. Within a very short period of time, if performance does not improve, there is sufficient justification to manage these employees out of the organisation (by following correct procedures in terms of country-specific labour legislation). Employees receiving a rating of 1 should definitely then be included in succession plans for employees who are considered as being high-potential and necessary to retain.

As these types of scales are not common, detailed labels and descriptors are typically designed to fit organisational circumstances and culture. An example of scores on an eight-point scale includes alpha ratings, which are indicated in the following table:

1*	2	3	4	5	6	7	8
A	B+	B	C+	C	C-	D	E

*Rating 1 is the highest rating, followed by lower ratings.

It can be seen from the above table that, unless very detailed guidance and descriptors are provided for line managers, they will have a hard time applying their judgement in terms of differentiating performance to such a level of granularity. It is often found that, when organisations implement these wide scales, they do not use the full extent of the scale owing to the complexities involved.

6.3.2. Alphabetical scales

In alphabetical scales, abbreviations or initials (eg "F" for "Full performer", "Ex" for "Exceptional performer") are used in an attempt to disguise the hierarchical nature of the scale. The alphabetical points may also be used to describe performance in an adjectival manner (eg a = excellent, b = good and d = unsatisfactory). In essence, the descriptors used for these labels are the same as those that would be used in a numerical scale.

6.3.3. Narrative method

The narrative method mostly used for performance assessment is the **critical-incidents** method. The critical requirements of a job are those behaviours that make a crucial difference between performing effectively or not performing effectively. Critical incidents are reports by the employee and other knowledgeable observers of things an employee did that were particularly effective or ineffective in accomplishing his or her job. Typically, normal procedures or average work performance are not recorded. The critical incidents so recorded provide a behavioural-based starting point for the performance assessment.

This method is quite time-consuming and requires dedicated team members, managers, clients and colleagues to assist in writing up the critical incidents during the course of a year. In converting critical incidents to a final performance rating, the incidents are classified in terms of a check list of required behaviours. On the basis of all feedback received, the line manager then indicates, on a scale, the overall performance achievement in respect of the required behaviour, for example:

Behaviour: efficient customer service

Strongly agree	Agree	Undecided	Disagree	Strongly disagree

Many organisations have adopted behaviourally anchored rating scales (BARS) to be used in association with the critical-incidents method. The ideal process for designing BARS is for a group of employees to first identify all the important dimensions of effective performance for a particular job. A second group then generates critical incidents illustrating effective, average and ineffective performance. A third group is then given the list of dimensions and critical incidents and is asked to locate incidents in the different dimensions. Incidents are eliminated if there is no clear agreement regarding the dimension where it belongs. In the final process, mean and standard deviation scores are calculated for each of the BARS, whereafter they are tested and finalised. The process of developing BARS properly is very time-consuming, and it is mostly for this reason that they are becoming less popular and less used in organisations.

6.3.4. Graphic rating scales

A graphic rating scale defines a number of factors or criteria, and the manager or rater is then asked to evaluate the degree for each of these factors that best describes the employee's performance on a continuum from poor to exceptional. In order to make meaningful distinctions in performance within dimensions, scale points must be defined unambiguously, which is quite time-consuming, but once it's done, it's done. These scale points are often referred to as "anchors" and can be in numeric, narrative or qualitative terms.

Graphic rating scales are popular with managers, as they are easy to complete and the templates are prepared for them in advance. These types of scales may not yield the same type of depth of performance as, for example, is obtained through the critical-incidents method, but they are less time-consuming to administer, permit quantitative results to be determined, promote consideration of more than one performance dimension, and are comparable across employees.

6.4. TARGET PERFORMANCE DISTRIBUTION AND FORCED RANKING

One of the problems with performance rating scales is that it is very difficult, and often impossible, to ensure that a consistent approach is adopted by all managers. It is almost inevitable that some managers will be more lenient or stricter than others. Another frequently mentioned bias effect in ratings is that of the Halo Effect. The Halo Effect refers to the tendency for some managers to use a particular aspect of an employee's performance to influence the evaluation of other aspects of performance – they could also rate an employee's performance on the basis of what they know (or think they know) about the employee, and not on what has actually been achieved. For example, a secretary's performance should be assessed in terms of, *inter alia*, her ability to manage phone calls, daily schedules, filing and administration, travel arrangements and client queries. If the manager has observed her being friendly and helpful with clients when she receives them, he would be making a halo error if he simply assumes that the secretary will be equally skilful and dependable regarding all the other responsibilities that she has, just because she has been observed to be friendly and efficient in terms of her client interaction.

Target performance distribution is also referred to as "forced ranking", which is an intervention where managers are required to spread the ratings of their employees on a predetermined distribution curve. This intervention is primarily used to reduce rating errors such as leniency and central tendency. Jack Welch, retired chief executive officer of General Electric (GE), is most often associated with forced ranking (a form of target performance distribution), since GE used this performance management tool to eliminate the bottom 10 per cent of performers each year. Many other companies have introduced forced ranking as a result of the success achieved by GE, notably in the oil and gas industry (64%), the technology industry (55%), and the consumer goods sector (50%). In a recent survey, 29 per cent of organisations indicated that they do not use forced ranking per se, but 53 per cent do use calibration sessions to address rating inconsistencies and ensure fairness and alignment of interpretation of performance scores across different business units or departments.

It can be argued that forced ranking is a tool that assists managers in accurately evaluating performance and in ensuring differentiation of poor and excellent performers. In many industries where collaborative team environments are important for success, forced ranking is not appropriate, as employees are compared with one another, often within and across teams, which results in a very competitive environment being created. For small teams of professionals who are all top-performers, forced ranking is also not considered appropriate.

Forced ranking generally has a negative reputation, with employees often feeling that they are not being treated fairly and have been "down-rated" owing to the distribution curve. It is also felt that employees will agree on a provisional performance rating with their line manager, only to be informed later that the rating has changed because of the forced-ranking process. This could lead to a culture of mistrust and demoralised employees, and to line managers not owning up to the final performance rating. However, in organisations where line managers are not adequately trained to conduct performance reviews in an honest and transparent manner, this practice could be used to ensure a proper differentiation in performance. Also, in business environments with a two-point or three-point rating scale which does not offer sufficient differentiation for purposes of incentive payments or increases, forced ranking could be useful in creating further differentiation and thus ensuring fair distribution of incentives and increases. Let the final word on this matter be from Jack Welch who stated, "Our vitality curve works because we spent over a decade building a performance culture that has candid feedback at every level. Candour and openness are the foundations of such a culture. I would not want to inject a vitality curve 'cold turkey' into an organisation without a performance culture already in place."

As an alternative, relative performance can be used in the distribution of incentives and increases, where the "pot" of money that is being distributed is fixed. This means that employees' performance ratings are compared with one another − therefore, if all employees receive an "Excellent" performance rating, the average incentive or increase will be that which an employee will receive if he or she achieved all objectives.

The following example illustrates this concept:

- Bonus pool to be distributed: 100 000
- Team: 10 employees in similar positions
- Target incentive: 10 000

Performance distribution:

Rating descriptors	Rating 5 Excellent performer in all performance areas	Rating 4 Achieved more than agreed objectives in some performance areas	Rating 3 Achieved all objectives	Rating 2 Achieved 80% of objectives	Rating 1 Achieved less than 80% of objectives

The following table illustrates how the incentive will then be distributed on a relative basis, without the use of forced ranking:

Employees	Performance rating	Relative incentive amount
Mark	5	14 706
Anthony	4	11 765
Rose	4	11 765
Simon	4	11 765
Tumi	4	11 765
Carl	4	11 765
Mary	3	8 824

Employees	Performance rating	Relative incentive amount
Andrew	3	8 824
Sarah	2	5 882
James	1	2 941
Average rating	**3,4**	**Total pool 100 000**

It is illustrated in the previous table that the distribution of performance ratings was not done on the basis of a normal distribution curve. However, by using this approach, the total pool of 100 000 was not exceeded and all employees received an incentive in terms of their own rating, relative to that of the average team performance. Further refinements can still be made and management can, for example, also decide to award no incentives to employees who did not meet all objectives.

If forced ranking is not used, calibration or peer review sessions are often used to ensure that a consistent rating approach is followed by all managers, and that the ratings of employees, also across different departments, functions and business units, are compared relative to what had been achieved. Many organisations hold workshops for line managers before every annual performance review period, reinforcing the interpretation of the different ratings and providing guidance for managers on the assessment of borderline performers.

6.5. ARE PERFORMANCE RATINGS DEAD?

Recently there have been a number of reports and articles challenging the use of rating scales and specifically, forced rankings and performance ratings. Some have gone as far as to pronounce "ratings are dead". The down side of performance ratings – numeric or degree scales – are that they can be demotivating, subjective and limited. This may be true, but it is more about HOW ratings are used, rather than the ratings themselves that is a problem.

As Rock and Jones[62] point out, many large companies have moved away from a simple rating system, towards newer ways of differentiating performance. These researchers found that social threats and rewards, like sense of status or fairness, activate intense reaction networks in the brain. This explains the intense reactions people have toward being assessed on a rating scale which focuses the brain on the rating rather than the message.

Rock and Jones[63] note that the trend to move away from traditional performance ratings is increasing and that there are clear signs of success associated with this move. They describe four main reasons why the trend is gaining in momentum and showing such success:

1. **The changing nature of work** – annual performance reviews do not take into account the collaborative team-based approach to work where people are involved in multiple teams, often spread around the world. The assessment of performance often involves matrix partners or team leaders who are not the direct line manager of the individual. In addition, goals often do not last for a full year in the new fast-paced world of work. Goals may need to be set weekly or monthly and they may change. Annual reviews are not agile enough to enable this type of performance.
2. **The need for better collaboration** – forced rankings have been shown to hamper collaboration. With many people competing for the top 15% of the rating scale, they stop working as a team and may even try to sabotage or undermine one another.
3. **The need to attract and keep talent** – development is usually formally included in performance reviews. When performance reviews are scheduled once or twice a year, development is only discussed in these sessions. Research has shown that when ratings are removed, managers speak to their employees about development more regularly promoting engagement and development, leading to greater attraction and retention of talent.
4. **The need to develop people faster** – when ratings are removed, people tend to have more frequent dialogues which are characterised by openness. Conversations are moving from the justification of past performance toward more future-oriented growth and development.

Why did Accenture Stop Using Performance Ratings?

In a bold move, especially for a company managing hundreds of thousands of people, Accenture recently 'revolutionised' and revamped its performance management process. In 2015, Accenture announced it would stop 90% of the traditional performance management processes that it said took up too much time, and were hated by managers and employees alike. But was the change as revolutionary as it seems?

From the headlines, it seemed Accenture was scrapping performance management totally – which is not completely accurate. In the past Accenture's performance management system prescribed that each employee be reviewed once a year using a set performance review process and specific documents. This process was time consuming and tended to focus on the paperwork rather than the person and performance. The process of performance management had not been adapted to the workplace or ways of work – for a company that worked on multiple, ever-changing, fast-paced activities, a static annual review was not appropriate.

It was nearly impossible to effectively manage and measure performance at one point in the year when most employees worked across multiple projects, with multiple people during the course of the year.

Accenture took the decision to retain performance management, but to measure and review performance more appropriately. They decided to conduct more frequent reviews following assignments/projects, and also to do so with less bureaucracy. This makes a lot more sense for a fast paced, agile firm.

Accenture also took a decision to scrap their performance rating system of forced ranking. In its place a system was introduced where each employee is rated against their own expectations and performance goals.

The philosophy of performance management at Accenture has changed to one characterized by development and 'instant' feedback and review as described by the CEO:

Performance management is extraordinarily important to get people to their very best. Do you feel good in your role? If yes, that's the perfect time for you to experiment with something new, to get out of your comfort zone. This willingness to learn is probably the most important thing for leaders of today and tomorrow.

Performance is an ongoing activity. It's every day, after any client interaction or business interaction or corporate interaction. It's much more fluid. People want to know on an ongoing basis, am I doing right? Am I moving in the right direction? Do you think I'm progressing? Nobody's going to wait for an annual cycle to get that feedback. Now it's all about instant performance management.[64]

Although most of the focus in the media has been on Accenture eliminating performance ratings, what is perhaps more instructive is their decision to adopt a developmental framework with frequent reviews and feedback.

There has been a large amount of hype about the 'death of performance ratings' with companies like Accenture, Microsoft and Adobe publicly announcing that they have scrapped the use of formal ratings. The question is whether this radical approach is sustainable and suitable for all. Research conducted by the Corporate Executive Board (CEB)[65] suggests that it is not as simple or as universal a solution as one might think.

CEB surveyed nearly 10,000 employees in their 2016 Pay for Performance Employee Survey. These employees were from across the globe, spanning 18 countries, and from a representative sample of industries and organisational sizes. They found that in companies where performance ratings had been eliminated, there was an initial period of "euphoria" where employee morale was boosted, but that post this period, reality set in leading to discontent. Employees became unhappy as they were unable to understand the philosophies behind pay and performance systems without the visible symbol of a rating. Employee engagement scores dropped 6% while performance dropped by 10%, largely due to manager inability to manage talent effectively without ratings.

Getting rid of performance ratings can only be effective when managers have the skills to have difficult conversations, are able to guide conversations about pay without a rating to "tie it to", and can communicate clear and effective expectations. This requires a significant investment in manager upskilling and coaching and even then, success is not guaranteed.

So what's the bottom line? Should performance ratings stay or go? The elimination of ratings in isolation is likely to do more damage than good. A sustainable change in approach which promotes a developmental underpinning to the entire field of performance management is a far better option. It is clear that the key levers of a successful performance management system include:

- Effective and agile goal setting
- Regular feedback from managers both formally and informally
- A constructive, forward-looking approach which is grounded in development and where the manager is seen as a coach and not an assessor

- Multi-source feedback including feedback from the manager, peers and stakeholders, and
- Elimination of forced ranking.

There are companies where performance ratings may have been successfully eliminated, but these companies are the exception, not the norm, and they have invested heavily in the coaching and upskilling of managers. For most, there is definitely still a place for performance ratings. As CEB very clearly states – do not get sidetracked by the ratings debate. Rather focus on manager development and enhancing the overall performance management system.

Don't kill ratings off just yet ... The Facebook experience

Facebook has discovered that when an assessment of performance is required, as it ultimately must be in all companies, it is how the assessment is made and not the rating itself that makes the difference. Even when ratings are supposedly eliminated and not written down, they are still made in "people's heads". When there is no rating to support an assessment, you run the risk that employees will find the assessment even more subjective as the criteria and scoring become vague.

Goler, Gale and Grant[66] conducted a survey in their organisation – Facebook – and found 87% of people wanted to keep performance ratings. Despite their downside, the authors said their benefits should always be considered:

- **Fairness** – employees want performance management to be fair, and many believe you need ratings to **show** the fairness. Employees are less likely to be disappointed with a lower reward or poor assessment if it is based on a rating. This is only the case though, if people see the process as fair.

- **Transparency** – employees want to be told how their contributions are seen in the organisation, they want to know how well they are performing. This could be done without ratings, but it is not always easy for managers to have the discussion without ratings.

- **Development** – Goler and her colleagues[67] argue that when ratings are not used, the time spent on performance management decreases. They also argue that performance ratings and reviews should focus on development, and that when one is receiving a lot of information as an employee, ratings help contextualise and make meaning of that information.

The authors say:

*At Facebook we are trying to build a culture in which people approach ratings with **curiosity and a learning orientation**. When our senior leaders receive performance evaluations, they often share the feedback with their teams, normalizing the fact that even people who consistently deliver strong results sometimes have lapses.*

6.6. CONCLUSION

In deciding which type of rating scale to implement, if any, some factors need to be taken into consideration, namely:

- organisational maturity and readiness
- employees' resilience and change-readiness

- whether the difference between the current and the new scheme will bring about the desired changes that are required, for example, introducing performance-based remuneration
- line managers' appetite for being involved in the implementation, and their willingness to be trained
- the integration points with talent management and remuneration processes and practices
- union involvement and negotiations or consultation
- the time of implementation and competing with other major HR projects

In conclusion, performance rating scales continue to be used in most organisations, as the advantages outweigh the disadvantages. Ratings can, however, be perceived to be largely subjective, and it is difficult to achieve consistency among managers. It is also at the point of arriving at a final rating where managers need to be clear that performance is assessed (and rewarded) in terms of what has been achieved in respect of performance goals, and that effort per se does not attract a higher performance rating.

However, if performance assessments are primarily used for development purposes and not for the distribution of incentives and increases, ratings can be dispensed with and the performance assessment can be done on the basis of qualitative feedback from management only, which should be duly recorded. The first step in establishing a performance rating scale supporting the performance appraisal process is to select the rating system that best serves the intended purpose and fits in with the culture of the organisation. Various types of rating systems have their own advantages and disadvantages. A critical element in ensuring fair and objective performance assessment is having trained managers who not only know how to conduct a thorough performance evaluation, but are also skilled in the drafting of the performance contract at the start of a financial year. Only then can an appropriate, well-designed rating system facilitate the process of eliciting satisfactory performance ratings that are agreed to between employees and managers.

Ultimately, for performance assessments and broader performance management to be successful, they have to be viewed as a business process and not an HR process. To improve a performance management system, an organisation must not only analyse the rating scales used, but also the key drivers of a successful system, namely leadership from the top and proper execution of the programme. Organisations getting the most from their performance management processes are typically those who are also hailed as top-performing organisations with strong leadership support and a reward structure that differentiates on the basis of performance.

6.7. BIBLIOGRAPHY

Armstrong, M. 2006. *Human resource management practice.* 10th edition. Cambridge University Press.

Armstrong, M & Murlis, H. 2007. *Reward management.* 5th edition. Hay Group.

CEB. (2016). *Understanding the impact of eliminating performance ratings.* CEBglobal.com.

Conger, JA. 1998. Qualitative research as the cornerstone methodology for understanding leadership. *Leadership Quarterly* 9(1) 107-121.

Corporate Leadership Council. April 2011. Performance management – survey findings.

Cunningham, L. 2015. *In big move, Accenture will get rid of annual performance reviews and rankings.* Retrieved from https://www.washingtonpost.com/news/on-leadership/wp/2015/07/21/in-big-move-accenture-will-get-rid-of-annual-performance-reviews-and-rankings/ on 22 February 2017.

Deloitte. 2015. *Rethinking performance management.* Deloitte.

Distance Learning Centre – online compensation and benefits education (chapter 14). http://www.eridlc.com (Extracted on 7 January 2012).

Goler, L., Gale, J., & Grant, A. 2016. Let's not kill off performance evaluations just yet. *Harvard Business Review,* November, 2016.

Grobler, P, Wärnich, S, Carrel, MR, Elbert, NF & Hatfield, RD. 2006. *Human resource management in South Africa.* 3rd edition. Thomson.

HRIZONS. 23 April 2009. Use the right rating scale for your performance reviews. http://www.hrizons.com.

McCormick, EJ & Ilgen, D. 1985. *Industrial and organisational psychology.* 8th edition. Michigan State University.

Rock, D & Jones, B. (2015). Why more and more companies are ditching performance ratings. *Harvard Business Review,* September 8, 2015.

Endnotes

56.   Armstrong, 2006.
57.   Corporate Leadership Council, 2011.
58.   CLC, 2011.
59.   CLC, 2011.
60.   CLC, 2011.
61.   Armstrong and Murlis, 2007 & CLC, 2011.
62.   Rock and Jones, 2015.
63.   Rock and Jones, 2015.
64.   Cunningham, 2015.
65.   CEB, 2016.
66.   Goler, Gale and Grant, 2016.
67.   Goler, Gale and Grant, 2016.

7 THE BALANCED SCORECARD APPROACH

7.1. INTRODUCTION

Since the introduction of the balanced scorecard in the early 1990s, organisations worldwide have not been the same. At last, it was thought, a reliable strategic planning, management and measurement tool was available. But there was, and still is, confusion for those rushing to implement the balanced scorecard without properly understanding how it works and how it affects organisational performance. For a business to achieve its objectives, it has to plan, manage and measure. The balanced scorecard is a tool that can do this.

7.2. WHAT IS THE BALANCED SCORECARD?

The balanced scorecard was developed by Robert Kaplan and David Norton based on a 1990 research study in the United States of America on balanced measures of financial and nonfinancial performance in manufacturing, service, heavy industry and technology companies. The research study was motivated by the inadequacy of traditional performance management systems, which relied almost exclusively on financial and business results. These measures were not telling the whole story. Their focus was mainly internal and based on single dimensions such as quality, cost or schedule. Although these were important, the limitation was that they told the story of only past events and were not consistent as regards the business realities facing the organisation. They were "unbalanced". The balanced scorecard helps organisations to link their strategic objectives to performance measures, and is set up to focus attention on matters of both internal and external concern. It is a management system that can be used by any organisation irrespective of size and purpose of existence to align its vision and mission with customer requirements, to improve operational efficiencies, and to build organisational capabilities (Makakane nd).

7.2.1. The balanced scorecard as a measurement system

The balanced scorecard allows us to view results of organisational performance from different dimensions, that is, business results (financial and customer), operations, and organisational capacity. It is based on the following framework of four perspectives:

1. **The learning and growth perspective**

    This perspective is about the organisational culture, tools, technology, infrastructure, skills and capabilities required to achieve the organisational objectives. It is essentially the foundation upon which organisational success is built. The measures in the learning and growth perspective are the enablers of all the other perspectives, as they will ultimately lead the organisation to achieve its results.

2. **The internal business process perspective**

    This perspective is about key business processes in which organisations must excel to create and deliver their value proposition to their customers. Measures based on this perspective allow the organisation to identify processes (e.g. new product development, more efficient ways of doing things) that are critical to meeting customer requirements.

3. **The customer perspective**

Organisations exist because of their ability to satisfy their customers' needs – the buyers of services or products. Customers can be external to the organisation or internal, for example human resources' (HR's) customer could be the operations department. If customers are happy and satisfied, they come back and buy more services or products; they also tell other people, who then buy the services or product. This virtuous cycle results in the organisation realising its mission and creating a sustainable platform for existence.

4. **The financial perspective**

For a profit-oriented organisation, this perspective is quite critical, as the financial performance provides the ultimate definition of an organisation's success. The measures in this perspective would typically describe how the organisation intends to create economic and sustainable growth, profitability, and rise in shareholder value. It would be of no help to improve customer satisfaction, increase operational efficiency and build organisational capacity if there is no measure in respect of profit making.

For a public sector/government agency or nonprofit organisation, the balanced scorecard focus changes slightly. Because a state-owned organisation/nonprofit is not profit-oriented, the desired outcomes centre on the delivery of service to citizens or on members' value for money. The emphasis therefore changes to the organisational mission, and the framework must be adapted (Makakane nd).

The underpinning philosophy of the balanced scorecard involves the linking of the performance criteria to strategic performance variables of the organisation in the first instance, and to customer delivery in the second instance. The following figure representing the balanced scorecard approach illustrates this linkage, with the four balanced elements surrounding the vision and strategy of an organisation.

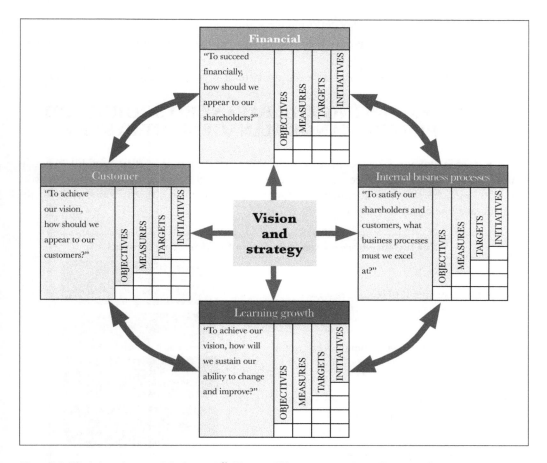

Figure 7.1: The balanced scorecard fundamentals[68] (Elegant JBI nd: adapted from Kaplan & Norton)

7.3. THE CASE FOR THE BALANCED SCORECARD AS A PERFORMANCE MANAGEMENT SYSTEM

The balanced scorecard can be used as a performance management system for the following reasons:

- The balanced scorecard helps organisations to understand their customer needs and customer value.

- It assists the organisation to focus on strategic results and strategy, and ensure that strategic objectives are linked to clear targets and the annual budget.

- It aligns the vision, strategy, processes, projects and people. As such, strategy is clarified, communicated and cascaded via business unit plans.

- It builds employee accountability and buy-in for change. The organisational initiatives are reprioritised and accountabilities, for everyone, are clarified.

- It assists in identifying critical performance measures and strategic initiatives. These are developed and linked at every level, thus ensuring that they are integrated.

- It assists in evaluating strategy performance.
- Stakeholder involvement is very high, thereby increasing commitment to making strategy happen.
- The balanced scorecard is adaptable for any kind of organisation, irrespective of size.[69]

7.4. IMPLEMENTING THE BALANCED SCORECARD AS A PERFORMANCE MANAGEMENT SYSTEM

To introduce a balanced scorecard approach, the organisation must first establish what its key strategic variables are. Once these are determined, each is linked to appropriate delivery variables, and, thereafter, to measurement criteria. These then become the foundation for the performance management system.

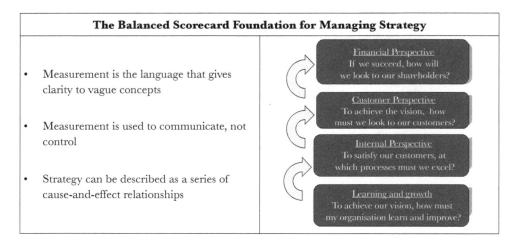

Figure 7.2: The four perspectives viewed strategically

Typically, the process begins with the strategic planning process, which will include aspects such as the vision, the purpose of the values, and suchlike. Strategy does not stand alone as a management process. It is a step on the continuum that begins in the broadest sense with the core purpose of the organisation. This, in turn, is translated down the continuum to the point that the individual actions of employees within the organisation are aligned with the core purpose. The output of the strategic planning process is a corporate strategy map as illustrated in Figure 7.3.

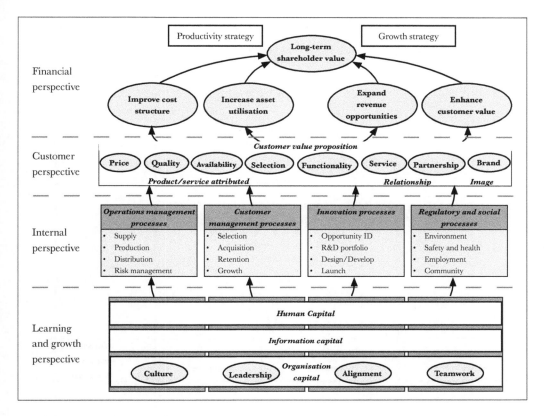

Figure 7.3: An example of a corporate strategy map
Source: adapted from Kaplan & Norton[70]

The corporate strategy map diagrammatically describes the strategy of the organisation. The map explains the strategy's hypothesis, where each measure of the balanced scorecard forms part of a chain of cause-and-effect logic. The development of the strategy map proceeds in a top-down way. The desired outcomes of the strategy – which are explicit in the financial and customer perspectives at the top of the strategy map – are then linked back to the drivers below in the internal business and learning and growth perspectives. These are the activities needed to create the desired financial and customer outcomes.

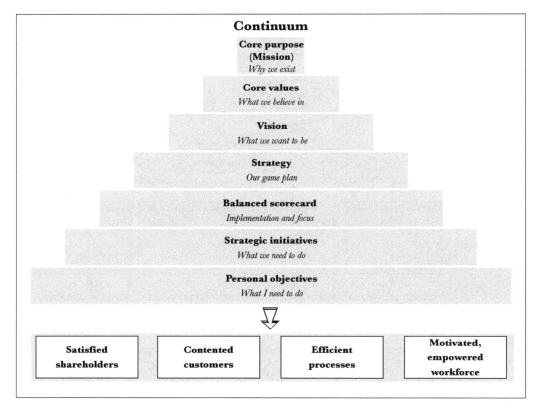

Figure 7.4: *Top-down structuring of performance variables[71]*

Built into the strategy map are two specific and complementary themes: **"Secure the Base"**, which is the focus on improving operating efficiency, and, thereafter, **"Build the Business"**, which is the focus on improving shareholder value. Ultimately, by securing the base and providing the operational excellence required, the organisation can then build up the business to provide the value proposition for its customers and shareholders alike.

In summary, the purpose of this strategy map is to provide a cohesive and systematic approach to strategy that management, staff and stakeholders can understand and identify with in order to drive the organisation forward.

Examples of vision and purpose for a typical organisation

Core purpose: To develop markets and facilitate trade for the benefit of all

Core values:

- Integrity above all else
- Exceptional service through attention to detail
- Innovative spirit
- Competitive
- Embracing a global mind-set

> **Vision:** As an internationally respected operator of markets, we gain our competitive advantage by:
>
> •   adhering to the highest standards of integrity
>
> •   being the lowest-cost service provider
>
> •   offering innovative technology solutions
>
>   We achieve this through our highly motivated and focused people.
>
> **Slogan:** "Building better markets"

The construction of the corporate strategy map leads as follows to the actual development of the balanced scorecard for the organisation:

•   Step 1: **Translate the vision and strategy** into tangible objectives and measures.

    1.   The essence of the balanced scorecard approach is to integrate financial and nonfinancial measures at all levels of the organisation.
    2.   The measures represent a balance between the external measures of the shareholders and customers and the internal measures required to drive the business forward.
    3.   The measures are further balanced between outcomes (results of past efforts) and the requirements for future performance.

•   Step 2: **Communicate and link** the strategic objectives and measures throughout the organisation in order to educate staff and align departmental and personal goals to the strategy.

•   Step 3: **Planning and setting targets** integrates the strategic plan with the budget and identifies the resources to achieve the required outcomes.

•   Step 4: **Feedback and learning.** The final (and the most important) step is to review the process regularly and systematically in order to continuously improve on the strategy.

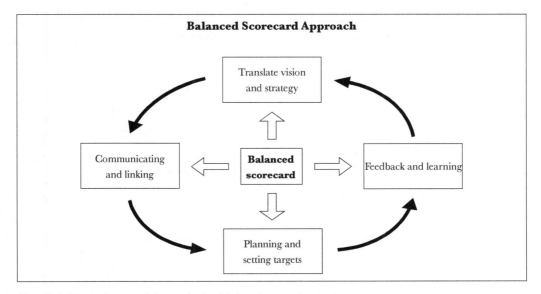

Figure 7.5: The development of the organisational balanced scorecard

The balanced scorecard provides management with a comprehensive framework to translate vision and strategy into a coherent set of performance measures. These are framed into four different perspectives. These four perspectives provide a balance between short- and long-term objectives, between desired outcomes and the drivers of those outcomes, and between hard objective measures and the softer, more subjective measures.

Once the scorecard has been developed, each of the perspectives has its indicators and accompanying measures attached for the period (be that quarter or year) under consideration. Typically, these are interrelated and can be depicted visually as follows:

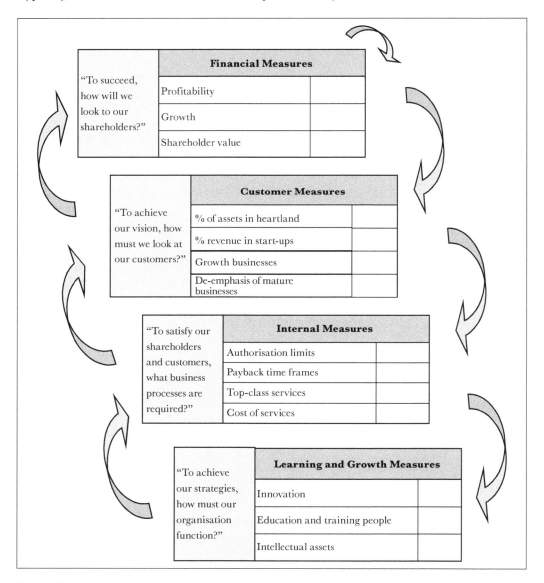

Figure 7.6: Balanced scorecard perspectives and indicators

An important consideration in the balanced scorecard methodology is that, although the original list of perspectives traditionally contains four perspectives, there is no reason why a strategic variable that is critically important to an organisation should not be added as a fifth or even sixth variable. If too many variables are added, however, the scorecard becomes unmanageable. Typically, such a balanced scorecard could be depicted as follows:

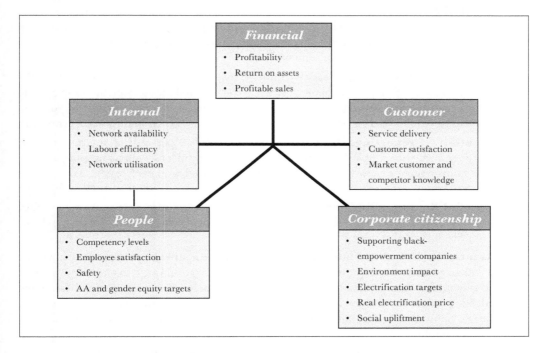

Figure 7.7: Adding an additional perspective to a scorecard

7.5. THE 10 ESSENTIALS FOR DEVELOPING SOUND BALANCED SCORECARDS

There are 10 essentials for developing sound balanced scorecards:

- **Essential 1 – clear objectives for the scorecard.** Why are you developing the scorecard? You need to understand that the balanced scorecard alone will not transform the organisation. Clear objectives are critical for communication, education, and guiding balanced scorecard evolution.

- **Essential 2 – executive sponsorship.** No scorecard initiative will survive without active executive sponsorship. Executives hold the key knowledge for balanced scorecard success, and everyone watches what the boss watches.

- **Essential 3 – a solid implementation team.** This is critical. No single person or group holds all the information necessary to build the balanced scorecard. Team members become crucial balanced scorecard ambassadors. Team participation itself is an outstanding learning opportunity.

- **Essential 4 – a strong balanced scorecard champion.** Such a person must be appointed at the outset. This person lives the balanced scorecard process, provides thought leadership throughout the balanced scorecard implementation, and should be committed, with the most time and job responsibility for scorecard success. This person must also be a good communicator.

- **Essential 5 – training.** The perceived simplicity of the balanced scorecard means that training is often overlooked. This is a mistake. Training and education are essential. The implementation of the balanced scorecard is simple but not simplistic – training levels the playing field and encourages involvement.

- **Essential 6 – the strategy story.** Strategy maps show the cause and effect of the organisation strategically. The balanced scorecard should tell the story of the strategy. The strategy map specifies the relationships and makes them testable. It also adds a powerful diagnostic tool to the balanced scorecard and is a great way to communicate the scorecard.

- **Essential 7 – reporting.** Don't wait until you have 100 per cent of the data to start reporting. Start with simple reporting tools and report results as soon as possible, such as at the management review meetings dealing with balanced scorecard results. Track action items and review progress. Use a banner scorecard as a tool for real-time strategic learning.

- **Essential 8 – cascading the scorecard.** Allow everyone to demonstrate how they contribute to the overall goals. Create a consistent language through measurement. Achieve a laser-like focus on strategy.

- **Essential 9 – link the balanced scorecard to management processes.** Show how the balanced scorecard has evolved from measurement to a strategic management process and system. Indicate how initiatives on the balanced scorecard provide a natural link to the budgeting process, and show how, by using the balanced scorecard, budgets are based on strategy. Show how linking balanced scorecards to compensation and reward makes it real for every employee. Remember that you get what you measure.

- **Essential 10 – make the balanced scorecard part of the organisation.** Don't think of the balanced scorecard as a project. Give the scorecard a home in the organisation. Develop balanced scorecard policies and procedures. Keep them simple and update the scorecard's core elements regularly.

7.6. CONCLUSION

The balanced scorecard is a management system used to focus and prioritise management energy so as to achieve both short- and long-term organisational goals, and with the ability to give early-warning signals for midcourse correction. The benefits of this approach can be significant. Done correctly, it draws on the knowledge that is widely dispersed throughout the organisation and integrates that knowledge to arrive at a strategy that best utilises all of the organisation's assets: physical, human, and intangible. Although the allure of a quick solution is ever-present, it takes time to draw together existing knowledge and generate new knowledge where necessary.

7.7. BIBLIOGRAPHY

Becker, Huselid and Ulrich. 2001. *The HR scorecard.* Boston: HBS Press.

Bhattacharya, N. 2007. Dividend policy: a review. *Managerial Finance* 33(1):4-13.

Carmeli, A, Shalom, R & Weisberg, J. 2007. Considerations in organisational career advancement: what really matters. *Personnel Review* 36(2):190-205.

Chang, RY & Morgan, MW. 2000. *Performance scorecards.* San Francisco: Jossey-Bass.

Elegant JBI. (nd). Corporate performance management solution – balanced scorecard. Retrieved from: www.elddegantjbi.com.

Estes, R. 1996. *The tyranny of the bottom line.* San Francisco: Berrett-Koehler.

Institute for Information Management. 2005. Seminar on Data and Information Management. University of Hannover. Retrieved from: http://www.iwi.uni-hannover.de/cms/index.php.

Kaplan, R & Norton, D. 1996. *The balanced scorecard.* The Antidote Issue 1:8-9.

Kaplan, RS & Norton, DP. 1996. *The balanced scorecard.* Boston: Harvard Business School.

Makakane, M. (nd). Tlho/ego Business Consultants. Retrieved from: www.tlholego.co.za.

Niven, P. 2002. *Balanced scorecard step by step.*

Painter, A. (nd). The use of the balanced scorecard as a performance management framework. Retrieved from: http://www.publicnet.co.uk/publicnetl.

Pike, A. 2001. *People risks.* New York: Penguin.

Rohm, H. 2003. A balancing act. *Perform* 2(2).

Rye, C. 1996. *The change management action kit.* London: Kogan Page.

Santonen, T. 2007. Price sensitivity as an indicator of customer defection in retail banking. *International Journal of Bank Marketing* 25(1):39-55.

Shackleton, C. 2007. *Developing key performance indicators for corporate communication in the information technology industry.*

Endnotes

68.   Elegant JBI nd: adapted from Kaplan & Norton, 1996.
69.   Rohm 2003.
70.   Kaplan & Norton, 1996.
71.   Institute for Information Management, 2005.

8 MULTISOURCE/360-DEGREE FEEDBACK

8.1. INTRODUCTION

Giving feedback on performance management is one of the more difficult tasks in organisations. 360-degree reviews were initially instituted for development purposes, but, as they have evolved, they are sometimes linked to performance. In the process, these reviews confront human resource (HR) professionals with a series of important questions, including whether to implement 360-reviews at all. This chapter explores the use of 360-degree feedback as part of the performance management process.

8.2. WHAT IS 360-DEGREE FEEDBACK?

360-degree feedback, otherwise known as multisource feedback, is a comprehensive and structured way to obtain feedback. It is a system or process in which employees receive confidential, anonymous feedback from the people who work around them. This typically includes the employee's manager, peers, direct reports, and, in some cases, customers or clients – in fact, anybody who is credible to the individual and is familiar with their work can be included in the feedback process. This is usually in addition to completing a self-assessment on performance. Each source can provide a different perspective on the individual's skills, attributes and other job-relevant characteristics and thus help to build up a richer, more complete and accurate picture than could be obtained from any one source.[72]

8.3. WHAT IS 360-DEGREE FEEDBACK USED FOR?

360-degree reviews were initially instituted for development purposes to enhance the cognitive process of self-reflection among participants, and increase self-awareness. As 360-degree reviews evolved, they have been modified to link to performance.[73] A 360-degree feedback tool assesses the contextual component of leader performance – that is, it assesses **how** leaders go about completing the tasks they do in their jobs, rather than whether or not these tasks were complete. Managers and leaders within organisations use 360-degree feedback surveys to get a better understanding of their strengths and weaknesses. 360-degree feedback can also be a useful development tool for people who are not in a management role, as it helps them to be more effective in their current roles, and it also helps them understand what areas they should focus on if they want to move into a management role.

8.4. THE BENEFITS AND CHALLENGES OF 360-DEGREE FEEDBACK

Using a tool to measure a construct for which it was not designed leads to problems with validity. One of the main criticisms of 360-degree feedback is that it was designed as a developmental tool and is instead being used to make remunerations decisions. When providing confidential feedback for the purpose of development, raters tend to be honest. When raters believe that their feedback will influence a peer's/manager's pay, the tendency is to avoid criticism and inflate ratings. There is also an aspect of game theory in 360-degree feedback when colleagues rate one another highly as a result of the "you scratch my back, I'll scratch yours" phenomenon.

There are a number of different types of bias that can occur when completing 360-degree surveys. Some of these are presented in Figure 8.1. below.

Contrast errors	First-impression bias	Halo/Horn effect errors
Employees' performance is compared strictly with that of other employees rather than job performance standards	Raters make an initial favourable or unfavourable judgement about employees and then ignore or distort performance based on this impression	Raters base their overall evaluations of employees on one positive or negative aspect of their performance
Range restriction errors	Recency errors	Similar-to-me bias
Ratings fall into the same general area instead of using the entire range available, thus decreasing the meaningfulness of ratings	Evaluations are based on one particularly good or bad event occurring close to the time of the review	Raters judge employees they perceive as similar to themselves more favourably than those who differ from them

Figure 8.1: Different forms of bias that affect 360-degree feedback

In addition to the challenges with bias identified above, 360-degree feedback is also not effective when it is not properly aligned with strategy, or linked to reviews and training.[74]

In terms of benefits, 360-degree reviews provide more comprehensive insight into aspects of employee performance and behaviour by compiling feedback from multiple perspectives, and enhancing individuals' understanding of how their colleagues perceive them and their work. The 360-degree review process reinforces desirable behaviours across the organisation, allows organisations to identify key talent, aligns performance with strategy, and facilitates positive employee change.[75]

8.5. TRADITIONAL VERSUS 360-DEGREE PERFORMANCE MANAGEMENT SYSTEMS

A comparison between traditional and 360-degree appraisal systems appears in Figure 8.2. below.

Comparing ...	traditional appraisals ...	and 360-degree reviews
How assessment is conducted	Lack agreement on performance measures and subsequently often overemphasise achievements rather than objectives	Ensure that supervisors and subordinates work from the same model of effective behaviours and outcomes by allowing raters to interpret performance measures

Comparing ...	traditional appraisals ...	and 360-degree reviews
Objectivity versus subjectivity	Raters and ratees each process a large amount of information from their own personal perspectives, leading to confusion and disagreement	Provide a broader range of information and perspectives, allowing supervisors and subordinates to view feedback in a more objective manner
Defensiveness on the part of assessed individual	Negative feedback causes individual defence mechanisms to protect self-image, limiting the utility of performance reviews	Reduce defensive emotions owing to increase in feedback sources; encourage open discussion concerning multiple perspectives and feedback

Figure 8.2: Comparison between traditional and 360-degree appraisal

The above table makes it appear as if 360-degree reviews are both superior and preferable to traditional appraisals. It is important to note, however, that this is only the case when the 360-degree reviews are conducted in an enabling environment where their main purpose is that of development. If used as a single measure of, or replacement for, the entire performance management process, the results of the 360-degree review will be falsely inflated and of very limited use.

8.6. THE 360-DEGREE PERFORMANCE EVALUATION PROCESS FLOW

The 360-degree performance evaluation process flow is described in the table below.

Definitions

Appraiser – the person conducting the evaluation
Appraisee – the person being evaluated

STEPS TO FOLLOW	DUE DATE	PERSON RESPONSIBLE
1. DEFINITION AND SIGN-OFF *1.1 Define KPAs according to the following categories:* ❑ Financial perspective ❑ Client perspective ❑ Innovation and learning ❑ Internal business processes *1.2 KPAs are broken down into the following:* ❑ Drivers (objectives) ❑ Levers (standards of measurement) ❑ Indicators (proof that outputs or standards are achieved, eg graphs, etc.) *1.3 Nomination of parties/appraisers* *1.4 Validation by section head* *1.5 Sign-off of the above*		Appraisee and section head

STEPS TO FOLLOW	DUE DATE	PERSON RESPONSIBLE
2. DISTRIBUTION AND UPDATING OF NEW APPRAISAL PACK ❑ Customisation of templates to the above requirements ❑ Appraisees to make copies per KPA subject according to number of appraisers ❑ Customisation of envelopes to reflect the appraisee and KPA (obtain envelopes from section head)		Appraisee
3. FINAL SELECTION OF APRAISERS BY SECTION HEAD It is the appraisee's responsibility to do the following: ❑ Obtain confirmation from the section head of the selected appraisers ❑ Inform the selected appraisers		Appraisee
4. DISTRIBUTION OF TEMPLATES AND ENVELOPES TO APPRAISERS ❑ These templates and envelopes should reflect the appraisee, selected appraisers, and scope of appraisal		Appraisee
5. APPRAISERS TO PERFORM APPRAISAL ❑ This will involve completing the required templates, signing-off, and sealing them in the envelopes provided ❑ Note that there is no discussion between appraisers and appraisee at this point		Appraisers
6. THE 1-ON-I APPRAISAL ❑ This involves the appraisee and the section head		Section head
7. COLLECTION OF COMPLETED APPRAISAL FORMS ❑ It is the responsibility of the appraisee to collect the completed, signed-off, sealed envelopes from the relevant appraisers, including the section heads ❑ These documents should be placed in a file reflecting the appraisee's name		Appraisee
8. HANDOVER TO SECRETARIES ❑ Once all completed documents are accumulated and filed, this file should be handed over to the relevant secretary: XXXXX ❑ A receipt should be obtained, from the secretary, as proof of submission of the documents		Appraisee
9. REPORT GENERATION AND DISTRIBUTION ❑ Capture the information on the Excel system ❑ Generate the summary reports and include in each file ❑ Distribute the file to the relevant section head		Secretary

STEPS TO FOLLOW	DUE DATE	PERSON RESPONSIBLE
10. PERFORMANCE REVIEW ❑ Section head and appraisee to discuss the score obtained ❑ Section head to facilitate discussion between appraisee and appraisers should any query over the scores arise ❑ The appraisee should lodge an appeal with the (relevant) senior manager should any issues remain unresolved		10.1 Section head 10.2 Section head and appraisee 10.3 Section head and appraisee
11. TRAINING NEEDS ANALYSIS/COMPILATION OF TRAINING PLAN ❑ Section head and appraisee to conduct training needs analysis as per the criteria indicated on the performance appraisal templates ❑ Section head and appraisee to draw up projected training plan for the period (start date – end date as per the requirements of the Skills Development Act) ❑ Access to database to be provided for each line manager by **date** in order to capture training plan ❑ Submission of training plan to HR by '**date**'		Section head and individual
12. PLANNING FOR NEXT SIX MONTHS ❑ Section head and appraisee to conduct KPA planning for the next six months		Section head and appraisee
13. SIGN-OFF ❑ Section head and appraisee to sign off the appraisal form and submit final score to HR by no later than '**date**'		Section head and appraisee
14. SUBMISSION OF FINAL APPRAISAL SCORES TO HR ❑ It is the responsibility of the section head to submit the signed-off final appraisal scores to the HR Remuneration Office **by no later than 'date'**		Section head

1-9 RATING SCALE

A common type of rating scale for 360^0 is the nine-point rating scale.
This scale will be used for all categories, that is, the following:

❑ Financial
❑ Client
❑ Innovation and learning
❑ Internal business processes

RATING	DESCRIPTION
SA (set aside)	For reasons acceptable to management, the position holder has not been required, or has been unable, to apply himself/herself to the job. Therefore, for the purpose of the review, the key responsibility has been set aside.
1-2	The position holder has not been effective in performing the job. Considerable improvement is required.
3-4	Although the position holder attempted to perform the job, the incumbent needs to apply himself/herself more effectively.
5-6	The incumbent is performing well against set objectives, and, in some instances, exceeds the set objectives.
7-8	The incumbent has accomplished more goals than the minimum required for acceptable performance.
9	The incumbent has achieved results that exceed the requirements in all areas, through an excellent level of diligence, commitment, dedication, and innovation.

SIMPLIFICATION OF THE 1-9 RATING SCALE

Another form of the rating scale uses percentages so that one can "count" performance. This gives the rating face validity, but this is not always possible to do.

GROUP	RATING	DESCRIPTION
Poor	1. Not at all	Only meets approximately 10% of set objectives
	2. Rarely attempts	Only meets approximately 20% of set objectives
Needs development	3. Sometimes attempts	Only meets approximately 50% of set objectives
	4. Almost adequate	Only meets approximately 80% of set objectives
Adequate	5. Adequate	Meets 100% of set objectives
More than adequate	6. Sometimes exceeds	Meets 100% of set objectives, and, in some instances (approximately 20%), exceeds expectations
	7. Frequently exceeds	Meets 100% of set objectives and generally (approximately 50%) exceeds expectations
Excellent	8. Almost always exceeds	Meets 100% of set objectives and almost always (approximately 80%) exceeds expectations
	9. Always exceeds	Meets 100% of set objectives and always (100%) exceeds expectations

8.7. 360-DEGREE FEEDBACK – IMPLEMENTATION GUIDELINES

Survey timing: The survey timing for the 360-degree survey is usually annually or twice a year.

Choosing the evaluation team: The supervisor and employee should mutually agree on the selection of the 360-degree evaluation team. The best assessments come from those people with whom each employee has the most contact. The team will ideally consist of the supervisor, colleagues, direct reports, internal customers, and others who are in a position to give credible feedback. Self-evaluations are also useful, and provision should be made for these.

The team should consist of a minimum of four respondents in order to safeguard anonymity. Evaluation teams larger than six are not necessary as they add to the administrative time taken to process results and typically don't provide new information.

Process design and safeguards: Safeguards are needed to ensure that the 360-degree feedback process yields fair and accurate information. Raters need to be assured that their input is anonymous and that no individual feedback receiver will be able to see how they rated. This will ensure that respondents are comfortable and honest in their ratings.

Feedback receivers need to be assured that their behaviour feedback is absolutely confidential and restricted to those who need to know, for example themselves, the supervisor and HR. You can ensure feedback receiver confidentiality and respondent anonymity by putting responses in sealed envelopes and returning them to the supervisor conducting the survey.

The 360-degree survey requires greater than 85 per cent participation by the selected evaluation team, failing which results will be skewed because of the small sample size of respondents.

Scoring safeguards: Scoring safeguards maximise the fairness of the 360-degree feedback information. To avoid substantial error, eliminate the most extreme high or low rating, as one outlier (ie extreme response) can skew the consensus score significantly. This error will most likely affect the highest and lowest performers – exactly the people for whom accurate measurement is most needed for both motivation and for purposes like raises and promotions.

To avoid the recipient focusing on the possible low range of a score, use a measure of inter-rater agreement on each item showing the degree to which respondents were consistent with one another. Invalid responses should be removed. For example, a respondent who is more than 20 per cent different from all other respondents will be statistically invalid more than 40 per cent of the time. There is no practical chance that a respondent is consistently correct while all others are wrong. This process will also remove obvious biases such as friendship, competition and collusion.

Reporting results: Reports should be simple and statistically sound. Feedback reports should be easy for users to understand so that they are motivated to accept and use the feedback.

Training on how to provide feedback: Research shows that participants who are trained in the process, including its benefits and how to give and receive feedback, are likely to support the process at levels between 70 and 90 per cent.

Training should ideally cover the following topics:

- What is 360-degree feedback, and why are we using it?
- What are my responsibilities?
- What are the competencies, and how will they be measured?
- What is the policy for selecting the evaluation team?
- How can errors be avoided when providing feedback?
- How will each person provide feedback, and when?

Training on how to receive feedback: Most employees expect uniformly high ratings because they have the opportunity to select who is on their evaluation team. Because friendship has little or no influence on the behaviour feedback, the scores are often a surprise

Supervisor-only assessments are typically significantly more lenient, reflecting most employees as good or very good. Multirater assessment tends to provide a much wider distribution of scores, and it reflects differences, both positive and negative, for feedback receivers. Because the average score is substantially lower than scores based on supervisors only, training is necessary to help employees understand the systematic differences.

Training should ideally cover the following topics:

- What is self-perception, and how is it different from others' perceptions?
- What is the value of feedback from others?
- How do I receive constructive feedback?
- How do I read the feedback reports?
- How will the results be used?
- How can I use this intelligence about me?

Create action plans: The feedback will highlight areas of strength and areas ripe for development. Action planning means developing a plan for making personal improvements based on this feedback. This action plan and sharing of progress will be shared between the feedback receiver and his/her supervisor/manager.

8.8. EXAMPLE OF A 360-DEGREE FEEDBACK SURVEY

An example of a 360-degree survey form follows.

360° Feedback
Business competence survey

Feedback for: _____ Date: _____

You have been identified by the individual being rated in this evaluation as one of a number of individuals who can provide valuable input for the employee on his/her performance. Your individual responses will remain anonymous (unless you are the employee's supervisor); only composite information will be supplied to the employee.

What is your relationship to the individual you are rating?
(Please fill in the appropriate square below.)

☐ **Self** …………….. "I am evaluating myself."

☐ **Manager** ……….. "I am evaluating the employee as his/her manager."

☐ **Colleague**………. "I am evaluating a colleague within my department."

☐ **Direct report** ….. "I am evaluating my manager."

☐ **Internal customer**.. "I am evaluating a colleague/team member outside my department."

☐ **Other** …………… "I am evaluating a person who does not fit in the above groups."

How well does this person perform this competency?
(Please use the following scale for your evaluation and then complete the attached questionnaire)

Not applicable	Least skilled		Not a strength		Appropriate skills level		A strength		An exceptional skill	
N	1	2	3	4	5	6	7	8	9	10

N = Not applicable or not observed

1 – 2   Least skilled. The individual consistently fails to reach behaviour and skill expectations in this area.

3 – 4   Not a strength. The individual meets some behaviour and skill expectations in this area, but sometimes falls short.

5 – 6   Appropriate skills level. This individual meets a majority of the behaviour and skill expectations in this area for the job. There is generally a positive perspective towards responsibilities.

7 – 8   A strength. This individual meets most, and exceeds some, of the behaviour and skill expectations in this area.

9 – 10   An exceptional skill. This individual exceeds behaviour and skill expectations in this area.

Customer service

☐   Treats customers like business partners.

☐   Identifies and understands, and responds appropriately to, the needs of customers.

☐   Presents ideas simply and clearly.

Customer service (continued)

☐ Listens actively to internal and external customers.

☐ Solicits and provides constructive, honest feedback.

☐ Keeps others informed.

☐ Balances requests with business requirements.

Teamwork

☐ Supports team goals.

☐ Puts interests of team ahead of self.

☐ Builds consensus and shares relevant information.

☐ Recognises and respects the contributions and needs of each individual.

☐ Actively seeks involvement/uses input from people with different perspectives.

☐ Builds and maintains productive working relationships.

☐ Treats others, such as diversity group members, fairly.

Business and individual skills

☐ Demonstrates broad business knowledge and skills.

☐ Acts so as to add value to the business.

☐ Recognises problems and identifies underlying causes.

☐ Makes timely decisions.

☐ Coaches and develops others.

☐ Is trustworthy, open and honest.

☐ Visualises the present and future, and develops strategies to get there.

Professional and technical knowledge

☐ Demonstrates professional/technical expertise.

☐ Improves existing processes and/or introduces new methods.

☐ Actively increases personal skills, knowledge and technology base.

☐ Makes personal expertise available to others.

☐ Organises work.

☐ Motivates others to achieve results by example and encouragement.

☐ Acts dependably to get things done right the first time.

Manages resources

☐   Takes initiative to make things happen.

☐   Takes informed, calculated risks.

☐   Makes well-reasoned, timely decisions.

☐   Follows through in order to deliver results.

☐   Uses resources efficiently.

☐   Communicates a clear direction.

☐   Anticipates and prepares for change.

8.9. THE ROLE OF TECHNOLOGY IN 360-DEGREE FEEDBACK

Increasingly, information technology (IT) software is being used to support 360-degree feedback processes. This has considerable advantages, for it reduces administration and allows the gathering of feedback where people work on different sites and in different countries. When gathering information in this way, particularly where the Internet is the medium, it is important to ensure that the process is secure and that the information will remain confidential among the agreed people.[76]

8.10. CONCLUSION

360-degree reviews provide a platform for addressing development by capturing feedback from others in a positive manner. Because feedback comes from multiple sources, individuals are more likely to accept this feedback, thus increasing the chance of employees adopting it.[77] As a developmental tool, the 360-degree survey has great potential and can be used for effectively driving performance and development in organisations. The danger lies in using 360-degree feedback for the purposes of performance evaluation and decision making for remuneration. Unless this is well thought out and included as part of a comprehensive performance management process, it is unlikely that using 360-degree reviews will be beneficial to your organisation or its people.

8.11. BIBLIOGRAPHY

CLC. 2006. *Considerations for implementing 360-degree reviews.* Corporate Executive Board.

Gray, S, Stewart, A, Anderson, B, Handley, C, Bray, D, Darling, P & Chivers, W. (nd). *Best practice guidelines in 360 degree feedback*. University of Surrey: Roehampton.

Endnotes

72.   Gray et al. nd.
73.   CLC, 2006.
74.   CLC, 2006.
75.   CLC, 2006.
76.   Gray et al. nd.
77.   CLC, 2006.

9 CRUCIAL/HONEST CONVERSATIONS REGARDING PERFORMANCE

9.1. INTRODUCTION

We've all been there before ... and we will be there again in increasing frequency in the future. You know that you need to talk to someone about work-related performance, but you keep delaying it and even avoiding it. Sometimes, you dance around the subject. Often, you resort to your best brand of humour, cynical gibes or, better still, caustic sarcasm, but the person seems to have a thick skin and an inability to get the message. On a few occasions when you were pushed to the limits of exasperation, you tackled the offender – resulting in defensive and disastrous reactions and a typical aftermath of a "no-speak" atmosphere! As a leader, you're good at your job, but you dread these conversations.

What makes our discomfort and inadequacy worse about not expressing our true feelings, speaking out and confronting reality are the intense feelings of guilt that they create. How often have we replayed incidents and exchanges in our mind, in the middle of the night, and considered the consequences and alternatives of standing our ground, presenting our view and having the courage of our convictions – in the moment?

It is not surprising that one of the biggest trends in performance management is the anxiety and ineffectiveness of managers and team players to hold honest conversations. People do not like any situation that could lead to conflict. Yet, every organisation is characterised by a pressurised work environment, in which bottom-line results are a function of the company's goals and targets, customer needs, supplier deadlines, performance standards, people management, and relationships. That's quite a crucible – especially when you add the other ingredients of personality type, cultural differences, diversity, generation gaps, power and politics.

9.2. HOLDING HONEST CONVERSATIONS

When things don't go as well as expected, how do we, as leaders and team members, address these important issues? Honest conversations should occur when the stakes are high and strong emotions are involved – a time when opinions, standards or expectations are sure to differ. People's natural reactions to many of these unresolved issues is to ignore them, avoid them or handle the conflicting viewpoint during a flashpoint of emotion. In today's world of high-performance organisations, it is imperative to confront the brutal reality by addressing, working through, and action-planning those unresolved issues.

Review the following situations. How would you handle these conversations?

A senior manager has been sliding backwards in his performance, never quite enough to be serious, but his personal effort and attitude are inappropriate and his half-hearted work is not going unnoticed. You know he has a "short fuse", but needs some direct, candid feedback regarding his contributions. You also know that the conversation will be potentially explosive.

A colleague of yours who you've invited to your project team owing to his special expertise is a "serial latecomer". On most occasions that you hold project review meetings, he arrives late, with a smile and an inane apology, and does not seem to be aware of his disruptive behaviour, let alone the loss of respect from the junior members of the team. You've approached him once before about the need for punctuality, but he dismissed it out of hand, citing his "pressurised schedule".

A customer has repeatedly expressed disappointment with your sales executive, as she feels she is not receiving the service that she deserves. You know that you should solicit her views and resolve her concerns, but your salesperson assures you that he is working on the relationship and you do not want to compromise the contract.

All three situations call for attention – silence and avoidance are certainly not the best option. You need to hold an honest conversation, confront the reality and get involved. The response required is engagement, and face-to-face dialogue. In recent times, leadership engagement has been referred to as one of the most essential practices of the transformational leader – having continuous discussions and reciprocal dialogue with direct reports, colleagues, customers, suppliers and higher management. It is essential that the leader not only masters the skill and process of addressing conflict and difference, but also creates a culture where all team members feel safe and comfortable in speaking out or challenging points of view. There is also often the need to hold honest conversations with your boss or other senior leadership impacting on your work responsibilities as a result of their leadership style, lack of strategic management or inappropriate values or attitude. These are always more sensitive and require both courage and a professional and accomplished approach in addressing such delicate matters.

One needs candour, boldness and accountability to hold difficult and crucial conversations.

9.3. TOWARDS A CULTURE OF HEALTHY CONFLICT

Change is about difference, and difference comes from different thinking. It is natural that, with the exponential growth of change in our work environment, the multiplicity of different views, ideas, expectations, understanding and time frames has the potential to heighten and increase conflict.

Honest conversations are needed in three general zones of problems:

Relationship breakdowns – often due to a breakdown of trust; often due to assumptions made and misunderstandings; often occur when relationship expectations are not met; when we feel let down, betrayed or disrespected; sometimes associated with feelings of loss – which provoke anger, fear or hurt.

Performance or behavioural problems – usually due to disengagement, lack of awareness or EQ, lack of skill in a new role, disappointment at work, an inappropriate attitude, abusive behaviour or loss of respect from team members.

Leadership style – often occurs when a leader's behaviour and attitude are in conflict with the organisational values, and when the leadership style is autocratic, risk-averse, noncommunicative, too operational and indecisive.

These conflictual issues, behaviours and attitudes require feedback, upward management and change, and there are real consequences that can evolve and spiral out of control if left unattended – ultimately affecting **your** performance as a leader.

It is often useful for you, as the initiator, to visualise yourself in the conversation with the opposing person, but for you to also stand back and take on a third-party (observer) role. This imagery helps you act out a mediator function during the process, helps you filter the past perceptions and emotions associated with this relationship, and prevents you from losing control when you are participating in the actual session. It is always so easy to get into the infamous "I am right, you are wrong" mode, and, sometimes, you need to practise some lateral thinking or seek some middle ground to resolve a stalemate.

9.4. FOUR PERSPECTIVES TO CONSIDER IN HONEST CONVERSATIONS

There are four perspectives that one needs to consider during the process of the conversation:

Impact versus intent – distinguish between the motivations for the discussion and what actually happens.

Story versus fact – the need to assess the facts of the situation under review against the distortion of perceptions and assumptions.

Loss versus gain – the need to review the implications of concession and compromise; the need to lose the battle in order to win the war.

Emotional versus rational – the ability to keep control of one's emotions and remain objective in contrast to being caught up in the "heat of the battle" and resorting to personal and subjective "blow-ups".

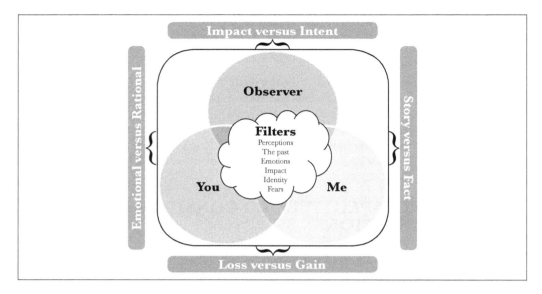

Figure 9.1: Four perspectives to consider in honest conversations

9.5. THE PROCESS OF INITIATING AND HOLDING HONEST CONVERSATIONS

There are a number of distinct stages and sequences for mastering honest conversations, including the following:

Purpose and initiation: The need for honest conversations and for tackling deep-seated and difficult issues is not a daily occurrence, so the initiation of this event should be handled in a fairly formal manner which also emphasises its significance to you. You need to consider the purpose and potential outcomes, to weigh up the benefits versus the consequences, to decide when and where to have the conversation, and to determine how you will set up the session.

With reference to the logistical arrangements, you need to invite the person for the conversation at a mutually suitable time, either in a written form or by talking directly to them, and to frame the high-level purpose and your desire to resolve any differences as a win–win outcome. It is also sometimes useful to hold the conversation away from the work environment at a neutral venue, and away from any disruptions and colleagues or staff interest.

Engage: As is the case in any coaching or mentoring situation, the first step in the actual engagement is to get the conversation off to a good start by building rapport, that is, by showing interest or offering a view on a common area of work, family, leisure activity, et cetera. It is also important to set the right tone, using eye contact and taking on a relaxed and informal conversational style.

The opening is important – explaining what happened, how you felt about it, and starting with all the facts as you set the scene. Always start with facts, not feelings. Your feelings are the least factual and often most controversial element. Remember the imagery of the observer watching over both of you: remain objective, show no emotion, and respect the "taking turns", reciprocal exchange of dialogue. The greatest skill to apply in this stage is active listening, without any interruptions – listen so as to understand! Watch the other person intently for any cues and signals that you can use to gain further clarification and on which you can build. Show respect during this initial exchange and acknowledge the position or defence that is being presented by the other party, whatever this may be. Remember that you need to be in control of this conversation.

Unpack: During this stage, you need to move deeper into talking about your feelings, about how you responded, about the influence it had on the team, about how the situation impacted on the results, et cetera. You need to unpack two of the process perspectives (loss versus gain), what you felt you lost in the altercation and what your original intent was compared with a description of what actually happened (intent versus impact). The skill of asking multiple open-ended questions is paramount in this stage as you seek to build a clearer picture of the issue, incident, attitude or behaviour that precipitated the conflict or difference of opinion. It is extremely important to gauge and assess the other person's response to this unpacking process, as it can provide significant information, viewpoints or rationalisations on which to focus. Again, use the skills of empathy and acknowledgement to keep the conversational flow, the integrity of the approach and the reciprocal exchange at a positive level.

Learn: So many clashes and conflicts occur as a result of different perceptions, assumptions, beliefs and past baggage that one brings to relationships. This stage requires discipline and flexibility, and the ability on the part of leaders to critically examine their own thinking, feelings and actions as a result of exploring the critical issue and broadening their awareness and understanding during the process. Leaders need to evaluate their own judgement, reactions, self-image and emotional responses in the relationship. It is in essence the honest conversation that you need to have with yourself as an after-action review, taking the wisdom and learning from the experience into your future.

Options: This is a critical stage in identifying options and alternatives for resolving the problem or topic. The initiator needs to facilitate this stage skilfully, and it is important that both parties enter into the spirit of conflict resolution, exploring the various options in an open manner as well as the consequences that need to be considered. Some of the areas of investigation include what both parties can live with and a decision as to what can be let go or sacrificed so as to move on. Obviously, there can be a wide array of options across the continuum of consensus – from forgiving, forgetting and reuniting, to slowly rebuilding trust, to agreeing to disagree and simply parting ways. Importantly, one needs to strive for an acceptable outcome, and the philosophy of possibility thinking can facilitate some positive future plans. The use of empathy and reflection skills can add significant value and integrity to the conversation, as one of the parties may have conceded far more than the other in an effort to move on.

Actions: The final stage in the process of mastering honest conversations is reaching agreement on specific actions to address the issue under review, as well as building trust and restoring the relationship. It is often useful to agree on the need to talk more and share expectations, which helps in healing some of the raw emotions that were central to the conflict. One of the commitments that can be entered into (in a case of misunderstanding or misperception) is to share thoughts and feelings earlier with each other, and an open invitation to ask questions to gain better understanding. There can be a host of different actions, but one of these has to be the writing up of the rationale, overview, outcomes and commitments from the session as a note for the record. There should also be an agreement on making time for coaching, performance reviews and regular feedback. The last feature of the conversation should be the initiator summarising the actions, accountabilities and time frame before concluding the session with a positive or encouraging review of the spirit in which the discussion was held.

9.6. CONCLUSION

Leaders are going to be faced with an increasing number of difficult and delicate situations, reactions and mind-sets in the future, and cannot avoid or distance themselves from addressing and confronting derailing behaviours, substandard performance and inappropriate attitudes. They also cannot "shoot from the hip" and then hope to achieve a professional outcome from a tough situation or emotive disagreement. The progressive leader needs to master the art and practice of holding honest conversations and to take on future leadership challenges with confidence.

10 PERFORMANCE-RELATED PAY

10.1. INTRODUCTION

High performance is a standard we strive for in all of life's activities. It implies doing a difficult thing well, whether personal or professional, and it often commands admiration and reaps rewards. The workplace is no exception and high performers often expect their achievements to be evident in their remuneration. Performance-related pay (PRP) is pay that varies depending on individual, team or organisation performance.

There has been some debate recently about not using performance-related pay. Arguments against it include the fact that it rewards risk taking and possibly unethical behaviour – in effect any behaviour to achieve the reward. Alternatives include capped pay, compensating behaviours and not targets, and making sure the measurement of performance is related to a balanced scorecard of measurement.

Equal Pay for Equal Work

There has been an increase in legislation that sets out a framework where work of an equal or similar nature, should be paid at the same level. The purpose of the legislation is to address discriminatory practices in pay. For instance, Ontario, Canada, has a law that requires men and women who perform work of a similar nature to receive the same pay. In South Africa, the Code of Good Practice on Equal Pay for Work of Equal Value has been introduced. This Code states that if work is identical; if work is interchangeable; if work is substantially the same or sufficiently similar to be reasonably considered as similar; or if work is of the same value when compared to another employee in a different job; then there should be equal pay.

It is increasingly becoming a legislative requirement to have detailed job descriptions, performance outlines and performance reviews. This is especially the case when one realises how much unconscious bias affects hiring performances.[78] Law is necessary to ensure non-discrimination, and structured performance management is required to be able to provide evidence when labour disputes occur.

We have just come through the debate of whether to ditch performance management ratings and now the next headlines are saying – ditch performance-related pay (PRP).

The main arguments of the proponents against PRP for suggesting this are summarised as follows:

1. **Performance may weaken if fixated on.** You may justify fixating on performance with the need to actually achieve it, but this is apparently the wrong way to go about it. Research has counteracted the idea of achieving performance by fixating on it, showing that focusing on the processes and strategies to achieve results is trivial. What works instead is structuring employees' goals around learning. In the 21st century, where protean careers (a concept that requires the employee to assess the job market, anticipate and quickly adapt

to an ever-changing work environment) are increasingly important to allow the employee to be resilient, education and learning prove to be of insurmountable importance and take preference over rewarding for achieving targets and attaining approving judgements from others. Expanding on a certain competence, attaining new skills and mastering situations prove to be far more valuable as they allow for something for an employee to fall back on.

2. **Only routine tasks benefit from contingent pay.** Performance-related incentives have proven to be effective for routine tasks but when the task requires creativity, this form of pay has a counter-productive effect. A study conducted whereby individuals were able to earn an extra salary for performing well that month revealed that their ability to accomplish the task was affected negatively by variable pay. In essence, when one's job requires innovation and creativity, flexibility and on-the-ball solutions to new and varied problems, variable pay is not the solution.

3. **Intrinsic motivation overshadows extrinsic motivation.** Intrinsic motivation refers to performance carried out due to the internal reward it brings the individual, such as a sense of achievement and satisfaction. Extrinsic motivation, on the other hand, refers to performance due to monetary rewards and the like. Contingent pay amplifies extrinsic motivation but jobs that require innovation and creativity rely on intrinsic motivation. Moreover, when extrinsic motivators are applied, intrinsic motivation is reduced.

4. **Contingent pay leads to trouble.** Lawsuits, earning manipulations and other such problems seem to manifest when remuneration depends on a financial measure as employees tend to be enthusiastic to maximise their performance no matter what, so as to increase their payout. Ethics are specifically compromised when an individual has fallen just short of reaching their goal.

5. **All measurement systems are faulty.** Incentive plans incorporate the use of a metric which determines the point at which the individual will be paid out but this is not an entirely smooth operation. Whichever performance criteria you base payout on will not be perfect and multidimensional jobs such as those of senior management are far more difficult to define.

Essentially, a person's behaviour will be compromised in one direction or another when linked with financial rewards. To help grasp the concept better, think of it this way: A company may reward its employees for completing a task and remaining within budget. However, if an employee has exceeded the budget, s/he might have been able to double profit as well. Thus, one performance criterion has hindered exceptional performance and the organisation will suffer unnecessarily as a result. Thus, such measures, although effective in one sense, will also distort behaviour on the other end of the spectrum.

Alternatives to performance-related pay

With regard to senior leaders, much of their pay is commonly tied to performance which has lead to a few questions marks for those who are not in support of performance-related pay. The reason for this uncertainty is due to the nature of their work as previously discussed. Additionally, there has been extensive debate, proceeding from the 2008 economic crisis, due to risky behaviour and short-term strategies having resulted from large bonuses and stock options. To avoid this, arguments have posited towards the reorganisation of executive compensation so that it encourages the right behaviour. Other proposals favour a fixed salary for top executives rather than the "controversial" performance-related pay.

The case for PRP

I believe that what gets measured and rewarded gets done. PRP provides focus and drives strategy. Most organisations implement incentive schemes in order to:

1. Incite superior individual, team and organisation performance.
2. Align with shareholder thinking (agency theory).
3. Share some of the wealth created in the organisation with those who created it.
4. Tie the onerous salary bill to the fortunes of the organisation.
5.   Reward participants for a job well done.
6. Drive organisation strategy.
7. Create more shareholder wealth.

The type of scheme implemented depends largely on what the reason is for wanting to implement the scheme. It also affects the scheme design, principles, measures used and targets set. It is a widely-held view that there is no one best type of scheme – the scheme has to be designed to drive the behaviour you want.

Some of the consulting giants like McKinsey and Boston Consulting Group[79] have conducted research which shows that organisations that have good performance management (PM) systems and PRP outperform those that do not. I support this research and wouldn't want to take the chance of ditching PM and PRP just because it may be tricky to do and some managers don't like to grasp the nettle of poor performance. Those who own their own business understand this perfectly.

Although there are many negative facets of performance-related pay, there are in my view far more positives. There are vast bodies of research which show that organisations which have financial incentive schemes outperform those which do not and, as the saying goes, "One person's poison is another person's cure." The next sections set out the possibilities.

10.2. INDIVIDUAL AND TEAM PERFORMANCE-RELATED PAY (PRP)

PRP which applies to individuals is associated with salary structures, grades and a performance and/or competence rating. This differs from incentive schemes, which are team- or organisation-based, as these schemes are normally formula-driven and the payments are once-off. In individual PRP schemes, a managerial rating often translates into the size of a pay increase relative to the "purse" that is available. The differences between team and individual PRP can be summarised as shown in Figure 10.1. below.

Individual PRP	Team PRP
1. Usually associated with managerial assessment of performance and/or competence 2. Payment is often in the form of a pay increase and is pensionable 3. Payments are mostly annual	1. Typically formula-driven 2. Payments are usually once-off and are not pensionable 3. Payments can vary from monthly to every three years

Figure 10.1: Individual PRP versus team PRP

Companies implement PRP for a variety of different reasons, but the most common objectives are to:

- strengthen the relationship between performance and reward
- drive the implementation of organisation strategy to individual level
- retain top performers by rewarding them for sustained, superior performance
- send a clear message to nonperformers (which is usually accompanied by counselling and/or training)
- instil a performance culture in the organisation
- facilitate and necessitate performance contracting, resulting in performance reviews and assessments
- link the onerous salary and wage bill to the fortunes of the business
- differentiate reward levels in a defensible manner

Research conducted by several major international organisations shows that those organisations that have well-developed PRP and performance management systems outperform their competitors on almost every measure.

There are three main ways to link performance to pay, and these are often driven by the performance management system:

1. Individual performance-related pay (PRP) – where you get a bigger or smaller pay increase
2. Short-term incentives – where, if you score well on your performance rating, you could get a bigger slice of the bonus pool
3. Long-term incentives and shares – where you may get bigger allocations and top-ups

The performance management system needs to be robust to withstand questions regarding pay allocations.

10.3. THE MECHANICS OF PRP

PRP is mostly driven by a performance management system, where a higher performance appraisal score leads to a bigger increase.

10.3.1. Application of reward or merit matrices

PRP can be used regardless of which performance management system is used, as long as the result of the system can be related to a ranked score for each individual. Once you have scores for each individual, or for the team (typically at lower levels), reward or merit matrices are applied to the scores. An example of a one-dimensional matrix is shown below in Figure 10.2.

Scale point	Performance description	Reward implication
5	Far exceeds job requirements. The employee's performance is visibly outstanding on a sustained basis and far exceeds the requirements set. Tangible evidence exists of the employee's ongoing achievements.	Deserving of a special reward or merit increase
4	Exceeds job requirements. The employee's performance exceeds the requirements set. Tangible evidence exists of the employee's achievements.	Should receive an above-average increase
3	Meets job requirements. The employee's performance meets the requirements set.	Deserving of the percentage increment top management sets for the organisation in general
2	Meets some job requirements. Requires further development. The employee's performance does not yet meet all of the requirements set. Some evidence exists of the employee's competence.	Should receive a restricted increase, lower than the average increase
1	Below job requirements. The employee's performance is below the standard requirements set. Little or no evidence exists of the employee's competence.	An increase should not be given, or only a very small one

Figure 10.2: One-dimensional merit matrix

10.3.2. Annual salary adjustments

The suggested steps and considerations in this procedure include the following:

- Key performance areas (KPAs) are weighted for their level of priority.
- Individual ratings are completed for all employees at least two months before the increment date.
- A summary of rating scores is prepared (at least one month before the increment date).
- A salary increase percentage is determined for the organisation as a whole.
- This percentage is allocated to the staff who meet the requirements set and who fall in the middle of the salary range for their grades.
- Suitable higher and lower percentages are calculated for employees who exceed requirements and are undergoing development in order to ensure that sufficient differentiation as well as the desired total salary cost increase is achieved.

- Lower increases will apply in the case of employees who have not met job requirements.
- Flexibility will be allowed by top management in determining final increments, especially in cases of very high and very low ratings, as well as in allowing for rounding off of salary figures.
- Closing of salary anomalies and gaps will be built into final increments after due consultation with departmental heads.
- Adjustments will not be finalised without reference to salary survey data and discussions with departmental heads.

The following is a guideline as to how the procedure could be followed, assuming an overall organisational salary increase percentage of six to eight per cent.

Scale point	Percentage increase
5	8% and above
4	6 to 8%
3	4 to 6%
2	0 to 4%
1	0%

Figure 10.3: Application of salary increases to performance scores (guideline)

The following remuneration review guidelines are suggested in order to assist with the implementation of the review:

- In addition to the above salary adjustment guidelines, it is important to remember that there may be a market premium on certain scarce skills in a particular area as well as on high-performing equity appointments.
- Employees who are not considered for salary increases, such as new appointments, should not be included in the review base. Employees who, as a result of performance will not be awarded an increase, must, however, be included.
- Earnings on equity dimensions must be monitored to ensure that an earnings gap, if any, is addressed and not widened. It is suggested that department heads complete a compa-ratio analysis (see the definition of "compa-ratio" below) before and after the review, by race and gender.
- It is recommended that the salaries of employees are positioned across the full spectrum of the salary scale. Employees who are below a compa-ratio of 75 and above a compa-ratio of 125 should be listed separately and commented on.

10.3.3. Definition of compa-ratio (CR)

"Compa-ratio" is an abbreviation of "comparative ratio". The compa-ratio shows the relative position of the employee in the pay range. For example, if the employee is earning 8 000 and the midpoint is 10 000, the compa-ratio is 80 (the salary is divided by the midpoint of the range and multiplied by 100).

Industry guidelines or norms indicate that an 80 compa-ratio is low and that there is a risk of losing the employee. Above 120 compa-ratios may indicate that the employee has a scarce skill and is remunerated above the norm.

10.3.4. More sophisticated merit matrices

A more sophisticated merit matrix has two dimensions. It shows not only the performance score, but also where an individual lies on the salary range or compa-ratio. Below is an example of a two-dimensional performance matrix. The percentage increase to be granted is reflected in the middle of the matrix.

Performance score	1	2	3	4	5
90th percentile (CR 125)	0%	0%	4%	8%	12%
Upper quartile (CR 120)	0%	2%	6%	10%	14%
Median (CR 100)	0%	4%	8%	12%	16%
Lower quartile (CR 80)	0%	6%	10%	14%	20%

Figure 10.4: Two-dimensional merit matrix

A matrix like this accelerates pay increases for top performers who are being paid at the bottom of the pay scale (or have a compa-ratio lower than 100). It decelerates poor performers' pay increases if they are at the top of the pay scale (or have a compa-ratio over 100).

There is an ongoing debate about whether or not to link performance management systems (especially 360-degree) to reward. Common reasons to avoid the link to pay and for first implementing a developmental-only process are set out in Figure 10.5.

New rules	Receiving feedback from multiple sources changes the rules for success. It takes employees a while to get used to the "new rules".
Competencies	The competencies used for 360-degree feedback are new and different from classic evaluation criteria. Employees need the opportunity to become familiar with these new expectations before they impact performance and pay decisions.
Training	Participants need to be trained in performance appraisal systems. A one-time use of 360-degree feedback as a developmental process gives everyone training in providing feedback as well as receiving it from others.
Experience	Using 360-degree feedback for development only gives everyone experiential learning in the process. Experience is likely to reduce participant anxiety substantially.

Refinement	A first project never seems to be perfect. Participant assessment from an initial process can yield insight into which design features to change or refine.
Low risk	Receiving feedback from multiple sources when the results do not impact on pay lowers employee perceptions of the "riskiness" of the new process.
Validation	Process validation occurs when value and credibility are established among participating employees.
Gaming	When participating employees have less at stake, they are more likely to provide honest feedback without trying to "beat" the system in their favour.

Figure 10.5: Reasons to avoid linking performance management systems to reward

The most common practice is therefore to implement performance management that focuses on development first, and then links it to pay.

10.4. CRITICAL SUCCESS FACTORS FOR PRP

Strengthening the link between performance and pay is a world trend. Some of the critical success factors discussed below are obvious, but serve as a useful check list.

10.4.1. Readiness

The following questions must be asked to ensure that the organisation is ready to implement PRP:

- Will it fit our culture and support the organisation?
- Are the top executives, and especially the chief executive officer (CEO), driving it?
- Has enough time been allowed for thorough communication and training regarding the new system?
- Are employees receptive to the process?
- Will managers "own" the process?
- Are there enough resources (human resources (HR) and/or consultants) to implement and do the training?

10.4.2. The system

It is necessary to ask the following questions to ensure that the system will handle the pressure and is easy to understand and administer:

- Do we have a robust system with good measures?
- Does our system support and drive our business strategy?
- Has the link to pay been clearly explained?
- Is the system easily administered?
- Does the system allow flexibility, especially in respect of the link to reward?

10.4.3. Support and maintenance

It is essential to be able to answer, in the affirmative, the following questions regarding support and maintenance:

•   Is there someone who will coordinate the implementation and drive it?

•   Can the system be institutionalised, allowing for continuous improvements to be made to the system from year to year?

There is no single best system or method, and, often, we allow the "paper" to hijack the process. It is more important to institutionalise the process and have meaningful performance discussions than to let a statement or score on a piece of paper detract from the performance review. Leaders must not use the paper as a crutch – it is an aid to what we are trying to do.

10.5. VARIABLE PAY AND INCENTIVE SCHEMES

The most common forms of variable rewards are normally described under the headings of short-term incentives (STIs) and long-term incentives (LTIs). There are many different definitions for these, but, broadly speaking, they can be grouped as follows:

Short-term incentives (STIs)

These are incentive schemes that reward superior performance over a period of one year. Typically, they reward what happened last year and look backwards. The main examples of STIs are the following:

•   profit sharing (PS)

•   gain-sharing (GS)

•   bonus schemes (BS)

•   commission schemes (CS)

Long-term incentives (LTIs)

These are incentive schemes that look into the future and reward superior performance over more than one year. Typical examples are the following:

•   rolling incentives (RI)

•   value-add schemes (VAS)

•   share schemes (SS)

Organisations should use both STIs and LTIs in their remuneration mix. The primary purpose of this is that it encourages the long-term viability of the organisation and executives are encouraged not to "rape" the organisation for short-term gains because they would have too much to lose in the long term. A well-designed total earnings scheme should prevent this from happening.

10.5.1. Implementation considerations

Implementing variable pay stands a better chance of succeeding if one uses the following headings to guide thinking:

- Purpose of the scheme
- Scope and eligibility
- Measures and targets
- Funding the scheme
- Sharing ratios
- Payment cycle
- Administration details
- Unhitching
- Claw-back clauses
- Dispute resolution

Is your organisation ready?

Ask the following questions to determine whether or not your organisation is ready to implement a variable pay programme:

- Does the business have substantial control over its performance?
- Have most of the major structural changes or system improvements been completed so that an effort to develop a new pay programme will not be perceived as a waste of time or overwhelming?
- Do clear, reliable measures support the existing strategy and long-term goals of the business?
- Is feedback on actual performance versus desired performance processed to employees in an effective manner?
- Do employees understand the measures and know what actions will lead to improvements?
- Are the current base pay levels internally equitable and externally competitive?
- Do the managers of the business consistently demonstrate leadership skills?
- Is the culture of the group characterised by trust, mutual respect, and a willingness to work toward common goals?
- Does the programme have a sponsor and a champion?

10.6. PAY IS NOT THE ONLY MOTIVATOR

It is important to note that performance related pay is only one motivator of performance. Intrinsic, internal motivations of performance are personal characteristics/preferences that must also be taken into account. Monetary reward is an essential and expected component of performance management, but other motivators of performance can be equally and sometimes even more powerful. Meaningful work, higher purpose, community development, self-mastery, and learning and development are all forms of reward that could form part of highly effective talent retention and performance motivation strategies. Including continuous developmental discussions as part of performance management is critical to make sure you understand what drives your employees and how you can reward them appropriately in ways that are meaningful to them.

Doshi and McGregor[80] speak about "total motivation" as a component of organisational culture that drives intrinsic motivation over salary and leads to greater retention and employee engagement. If employees have a clearly understood value and purpose in the organisation they will be more strongly motivated. Less effective motivators include emotional pressure to stay in a job, fear of punishment, and economic pressures. It is true that a business cannot operate without financial rewards and recognition, but it is important to include other motivators.

10.7. CONCLUSION

One of the main responsibilities of management is to try to optimise the organisation's remuneration system. On the one hand, it is necessary to do everything possible to retain good employees, necessitating a focus on employee motivation and satisfaction. On the other, it is important to make sure that employees' pay is in relation to their productivity and is linked to organisation success. A total remuneration strategy is required to ensure that performance is maximised in a sustainable manner.

10.8. BIBLIOGRAPHY

Boston Consulting Group, Realizing the Value of People Management. Retrieved from https://www.bcgperspectives. com/content/articles/people_management_human_resources_leadership_from_capability_to_ profitability/?chapter=3 31 March 2017.

Doshi, N. & McGregor, L. (2015). *Primed to perform*. USA: HarperCollins.

Ewenstein, B., Hancock, B., and Komm, A. 'Ahead of the curve: The future of performance management'. *McKinsey Quarterly*, May 2016. Retrieved from: www.mckinsey.com/business-functions/organization/our-insights/ahead-of-the-curve-the-future-of-performance-management

Parrado, E. (2016). What the banking world reveals about unconscious bias. *World Economic Forum*, September 23, 2016.

Endnotes

78.   Parrado, 2016.
79.   Ewenstein et al. 2016 and Boston Consulting Group, 2017
80.   Doshi & McGregor, 2015.

11 THE LINK BETWEEN PERFORMANCE MANAGEMENT AND LONG-TERM INCENTIVES (LTIS)

11.1. INTRODUCTION

The definition of performance is simple and is as viewed by shareholders. It is the increase in the value of the company's shares together with dividends received over time. This is termed total shareholder return (TSR). Shareholders often value TSR either with reference to one or more indices or an arbitrary measure such as the interest rate on cash, plus the consumer price index (CPI), plus a factor for risk.

The link between performance management and share-based, long-term incentives (LTIs) is simple in its essence. It is based on the fundamental premise that top executives are able, through their employment, to conduct the company's affairs in such a manner as to influence the company's share price favourably, and will do so if:

- sufficient LTIs are awarded to them, and
- the LTIs vest over a sufficient period in order to ensure sustained positive share price performance, and thereby also ensure the retention of the executives.

11.2. QUANTA OF LTIs AWARDED TO EXECUTIVES

11.2.1 Quanta awarded in South Africa

LTI equity award quanta are typically determined by two distinct factors:

Whether the award of equity is in the form of:

A. "Growth/Appreciation" shares, where participants only benefit from the growth in the value of the share between award date and vesting date eg Options, SARs, or

B. "Full Value/Free" shares, where participants benefit from the full value of the share, even if such value decreases between the award date and the vesting date eg Restricted or Performance Shares.

We now provide **overall JSE Market Data on LTI award quanta**, where top-ups are made at vesting, as well as where annual awards are made. It should be noted that:

- the quanta shown represent where the full allocation is made in that particular award type;
- the quanta are expressed as a multiple of current Total Guaranteed Package;
- it is market practice that equity that has already vested (but not yet exercised) is not taken into account when considering the quantum of new allocations. The reason is that, once equity has vested, it holds no retention value, and if the Executive chooses not to exercise, it is purely an "investment" decision and not an "employment" decision.

A.   Growth Shares with Top-Ups at Vesting

Table 11.1: LTI Award Multiples – Growth Shares with Top-Ups at Vesting[81]

Strategic Level	Typical Title	Paterson Grade	P10	P25	P50	P75	P90
Top Management; Strategic Intent	Group CEO	F Upper	0.98	2.89	8.71	19.41	33.87
	CEO/MD; Subsidiary CEO/MD; Group Functional Director	F Lower	0.59	2.57	6.23	13.69	23.20
General Management; Strategic Execution	CEO/MD; Subsidiary CEO/MD; Functional Director	E Upper	0.44	1.93	4.72	10.78	20.17
Senior Management; Strategic Execution	Functional Director	E Lower	0.35	1.54	3.78	8.36	17.09
Middle Management; Qualified Professionals; Experienced Professionals	Supervisor, Foreman, Superintendent	D	0.29	1.28	2.84	4.78	12.38
Advanced Operational; Skilled Technical; Academically Qualified; Junior Management		C	0.15	0.64	1.51	2.86	6.19
Operational & Primary; Semi and Unskilled		B, A	0.15	0.64	1.32	2.38	5.25

B. Full Value Shares with Top-Ups at Vesting

Table 11.2: LTI Award Multiples – Full Value Shares with Top-Ups at Vesting

Strategic Level	Typical Title	Paterson Grade	P10	P25	P50	P75	P90
Top Management; Strategic Intent	Group CEO	F Upper	0.25	0.73	2.21	4.93	8.60
	CEO/MD; Subsidiary CEO/MD; Group Functional Director	F Lower	0.15	0.65	1.58	3.48	5.89
General Management; Strategic Execution	CEO/MD; Subsidiary CEO/MD; Functional Director	E Upper	0.11	0.49	1.20	2.74	5.12
Senior Management; Strategic Execution	Functional Director	E Lower	0.09	0.39	0.96	2.12	4.34
Middle Management; Qualified Professionals; Experienced Professionals	Supervisor, Foreman, Superintendent	D	0.08	0.33	0.72	1.21	3.14
Advanced Operational; Skilled Technical; Academically Qualified; Junior Management		C	0.04	0.17	0.38	0.72	1.57
Operational & Primary; Semi and Unskilled		B, A	0.04	0.17	0.33	0.60	1.33

C. Annual Awards of Growth Shares

Table 11.3: LTI Award Multiples – Growth Shares Awarded Annually

Strategic Level	Typical Title	Paterson Grade	P10	P25	P50	P75	P90
Top Management; Strategic Intent	Group CEO	F Upper	0.31	0.95	2.92	6.46	11.30
	CEO/MD; Subsidiary CEO/MD; Group Functional Director	F Lower	0.20	0.87	2.09	4.56	7.72
General Management; Strategic Execution	CEO/MD; Subsidiary CEO/MD; Functional Director	E Upper	0.16	0.67	1.57	3.58	6.70
Senior Management; Strategic Execution	Functional Director	E Lower	0.12	0.55	1.26	2.80	5.67
Middle Management; Qualified Professionals; Experienced Professionals	Supervisor, Foreman, Superintendent	D	0.11	0.47	0.95	1.62	4.10
Advanced Operational; Skilled Technical; Academically Qualified; Junior Management		C	0.08	0.23	0.52	0.99	2.05
Operational & Primary; Semi and Unskilled		B, A	0.08	0.23	0.44	0.83	1.74

D. Annual Awards of Full Value Shares

Table 11.4: LTI Award Multiples – Cash/Full Value Shares Awarded Annually

Strategic Level	Typical Title	Paterson Grade	P10	P25	P50	P75	P90
Top Management; Strategic Intent	Group CEO	F Upper	0.08	0.24	0.74	1.64	2.87
	CEO/MD; Subsidiary CEO/MD; Group Functional Director	F Lower	0.05	0.22	0.53	1.16	1.96
General Management; Strategic Execution	CEO/MD; Subsidiary CEO/MD; Functional Director	E Upper	0.04	0.17	0.40	0.91	1.70
Senior Management; Strategic Execution	Functional Director	E Lower	0.03	0.14	0.32	0.71	1.44
Middle Management; Qualified Professionals; Experienced Professionals	Supervisor, Foreman, Superintendent	D	0.03	0.12	0.24	0.41	1.04
Advanced Operational; Skilled Technical; Academically Qualified; Junior Management		C	0.02	0.06	0.13	0.25	0.52
Operational & Primary; Semi and Unskilled		B, A	0.02	0.06	0.11	0.21	0.44

The market will typically use **growth shares** to drive **performance** and **full value** shares to manage **retention** of key staff. The King Reports on Governance for South Africa acknowledges the dual role played by LTIs in driving an organisation's performance while also serving as a retention mechanism.

The data provides no reflection of growth in the value of the benefit to participants over time, as this is influenced materially by:

* growth in the value of each company's share price
* tax structuring of schemes
* vesting terms and conditions

Best governance principles suggest that allocations be made annually in even quanta to reach the target multiples, rather than in one large quantum. This is to guard against overcompensation from awarding shares or options in large quanta when share prices are at a low. It is usual practice that allocations be spread evenly over three years to reach the target multiples for each participant.

A full share, share option or appreciation right can only have an absolute value once it is capable of being exercised and delivered (ie when the price of the underlying share is known and confirmed). Because the delivery and/or exercise dates are in the future, the Black–Scholes model attempts to place a value on the shares at the dates in the future when delivery can be effected, and it discounts that future value to a present value.

The following table gives an indication of the LTI values as a percentage of guaranteed packages using the Black–Scholes evaluation in current market conditions.

Table 11.5: Annualised LTI values in South Africa as a percentage of guaranteed package (Source: 21st Century)

Decision-making level	Eligibility*	Typical Paterson Grade	Typical roles	Annual value as a % of guaranteed package		
				Lower Quartile	Median	Upper Quartile
Top management; strategic intent	90%	F Upper	Group CEO	56%	83%	111%
	85%	F Lower	CEO/MD; subsidiary CEO/MD; Group Functional Director	28%	56%	97%
General management; strategic execution	80%	E Upper	CEO/MD; subsidiary CEO/MD; Functional Director	21%	42%	69%
Senior management; strategic execution	70%	E Lower	Functional Director	14%	28%	42%

Various assumptions need to be made in using the Black–Scholes model and in calculating the value of a participating executive's options. The following assumptions have been made in this example:

- The risk-free interest rate used to discount future values is 11%.
- In statistically predicting what the company's share price will be at certain dates in the future, a volatility factor of 30% was used.
- Only unvested options were valued.
- Performance hurdles were assumed to be met.

The assumed vesting schedule is as follows:

- 33,3% in year 3
- 33,3% in year 4
- 33,3% in year 5

We assumed top-ups upon vesting.

Once the absolute value of the shares has been determined, we calculated an annual net present value of the shares. This was done by dividing the total net present value by the number of years before the shares vest, in order to arrive at an annual value for the shares (either full shares or appreciation).

As an example, a CEO with 6x multiple of fixed remuneration package = 83% of package annualised using these assumptions per the table above.

Please note that this is a theoretical model as it assumes performance into the future. In years when the market is offering excellent returns (or vice versa) the results could be quite different.

11.2.2. Quanta awarded in the United States of America

The key trends include the following:

- Ownership policy prevalence: The prevalence of Fortune 100 companies with publicly disclosed executive stock policies increased.
- Ownership guideline prevalence: Boosted by an overall increase in ownership policies, the prevalence of ownership guidelines at Fortune 100 companies increased.
- Holding requirement prevalence: Like ownership guidelines, the prevalence of holding requirements at Fortune 100 companies increased.
- Ownership guideline design: Executive stock ownership guidelines defining stock ownership targets as a multiple of base salary are still the most commonly used design model.
- CEO target ownership levels: At Fortune 100 companies the median value of target ownership levels for CEOs was approximately 1x annual salary.
- Allocation values: The median value of base salary allocation multiples for top executive positions ranged from 4x to 5x.
- Accumulation periods: most specified an accumulation period of 5 years.

11.3. VESTING PERIODS

11.3.1 The specific vesting periods in South Africa

Table 11.6: Market practice – vesting periods for LTIs in South Africa (Source: 21ˢᵗ Century)

Vesting periods	Result
Range of vesting periods:	3 to 10 years
3 years	22%
4 years	6%
5 years	42%
6 years	5%
7-10 years	25%

However, corporate governance requirements from the recent King IV report on corporate governance state that share options or other conditional share awards are normally granted for the year in question and in expectation of service over a performance measurement period of not less than 3 years. Accordingly, shares and options should not vest or be exercisable within 3 years from the date of grant. In addition, options should not be exercisable more than 10 years from the date of grant.

11.4. CONSIDERATIONS IN ALLOCATING LTIs – LINK TO PERFORMANCE

Target allocation multiples for share-based LTIs are most often determined primarily with reference to the job grades of participants. Typically, the LTI allocation multiples of annual fixed remuneration packages will increase for higher job grades according to market criteria. These tend to be weighted in terms of the size of the employer company and are typically represented in quartiles. This implicitly forms a representation of the participants' participation to the degree that the job grading system is representative of participation. A sound job grading system would reflect the size of the job as well as its compexity and relevance of the required outputs to the organisation's overall success – hence a link to performance through these outputs.

The participant's current actual performance and value to the company, and future value to the organisation or potential, would not be reflected by the job grading system. Consequently, a prudent employer would determine LTI allocation multiples by combining the job grading system as described above with the measures of the participant's current performance levels from the performance management system to assess the participant's current value to the company. This could further be weighted by reflecting on the future value of the participant given his or her role per the company's management succession structure and planning for execution of the company's strategy. The table below reflects a typical matrix for this purpose, where higher scores reflect larger LTI allocations and scores of say two or less would receive, say, zero allocations.

FUTURE	HIGH	3	5	7
VALUE/	MEDIUM	2	3	4
POTENTIAL	LOW	0	1	2
		LOW	MEDIUM	HIGH
		CURRENT	VALUE / PERFORMANCE	CONTRIBUTION

Figure 11.1: Example of an allocation matrix for LTIs

11.5. SPECIFIC PERFORMANCE CONDITIONS APPLICABLE TO LTIs

Most LTI schemes in South Africa are designed in line with the premise that aligning executive interests with those of shareholders is a paramount consideration. This is commonly interpreted to mean that the same benefits conferring on shareholders (in terms of growth in the share price) should accrue to participants. However, the main concern in this regard is that executives should not benefit from growth in the share price where external factors (such as a weakening rand for companies that export their product) have influenced the share price, especially in cases where the intrinsic performance of such companies might have weakened (e.g. in terms of cost management or decreased market share). The argument is exacerbated when executives contrive to issue shares at the point where a high probability of favourable external circumstances can readily be foreseen.

In the United Kingdom, institutional investors from the Association of British Insurers (ABI) have brought their influence to bear on United Kingdom listed companies by issuing guidelines that deal with the above concerns as follows:

- Equity should be issued on a regular basis (annually) to counter the effect of external factors on benefits. This would mean that, if an issue multiple of 5x guaranteed package is agreed, then equity to the value of, say, 1x guaranteed package should be issued annually over a period of five years.

- Performance hurdles should be tied either to the awarding or to the vesting conditions. These should be designed so that benefits confer according to the successful implementation of factors within management's control. Typically, the measures could be return on equity in excess of a hurdle rate or returns in excess of those achieved by a peer group of companies.

We agree with the notion that incentive plan design can influence the effectiveness of share schemes to achieve the following goals:

- align executive compensation with shareholder interests and the long-term success of a company, and

- attract and retain executive talent by offering competitive compensation.

Internationally, First World organisations commonly use TSR as a performance metric for executive share scheme compensation. Companies may also use other performance metrics in addition to, or in lieu of, TSR, for example Earnings Per Share and Profit measures. The usage of multiple metrics allows companies to target multiple performance goals, clearly linking incentives to business strategy.

Economic performance metrics tend to take on financial metrics as shown in Table 11.7[82] for the S&P 500 and the industry sectors. It can be seen that relative TSR is the most commonly used measure. However numerous studies have shown that relative TSR is not a reliable measure of sustainable performance.

Table 11.7: Performance metrics in USA

SECTOR	METRIC	PREVALENCE
S&P 500	Relative TSR	47.8%
	EPS	25.3%
	Revenue	22.1%
Basic Materials	Relative TSR	68.1%
	ROC/ROIC	33.6%
	Cash Flow	10.6%
	EBITDA	10.6%
Consumer Goods	Relative TSR	38.0%
	EPS	32.4%
	Revenue	31.5%
Financial	Relative TSR	50.0%
	ROE	28.4%
	EPS	25.3%
Healthcare	Relative TSR	48.0%
	EPS	37.3%
	Revenue	30.7%
Industrial Goods	Relative TSR	45.3%
	ROC/ROIC	27.4%
	EPS	25.5%
Services	Relative TSR	30.5%
	Revenue	28.6%
	Operating Income	27.7%
Technology	Relative TSR	45.9%
	EPS	43.9%
	Operating Income	27.7%
Utilities	Relative TSR	93.0%
	EPS	33.3%
	Net Income	14.0%
	ROE	14.0%

Some companies have linked vesting of shares to individual performance as well, but, more commonly, a disqualifier is in place to disqualify participants whose performance is below a certain level. In these instances it is important to have a robust performance system for individuals.

11.6. CONCLUSION

Companies have moved to a stronger link between LTIs and performance at allocation, rather than using a level-based approach. In addition, the link between LTIs at allocation and at vesting has become stronger in recent years using company and individual measures.

11.7. BIBLIOGRAPHY

Equilar Blog. 2015. Weighing in on Performance Metrics. August 27, 2015 http://www.equilar.com/blogs/44-weighing-in-on-performance-metrics.html retrieved 31 March 2017.

Endnotes

81   Equilar Blog, 2015
82   Equilar Blog, 2015

12 DIRECTOR AND BOARD EVALUATIONS

12.1. INTRODUCTION

This chapter is about board and director evaluations. It describes the rationale for evaluations, provides an overview of the legislation regarding evaluations, and indicates the steps and processes to develop and implement effective evaluations.[83] Evaluations should not be academic exercises. They should help identify and address corporate governance gaps,[84] thereby improving corporate performance and ensuring the long-term sustainability of the organisation.

12.2. CORPORATE GOVERNANCE DEFINED

Corporate governance is the system by which companies are directed and controlled.[85] Boards of directors are responsible for the governance of their companies. The shareholders' role in governance is to appoint the directors and the auditors, and to satisfy themselves that an appropriate governance structure is in place. The responsibilities of the board include setting the company's strategic aims, providing the leadership to put them into effect, supervising the management of the business,[86] and reporting to shareholders on their stewardship.[87] The board's actions are subject to laws and regulations, and to the shareholders in a general meeting.

Good corporate governance is essential for any organisation's long-term growth and sustainability.[88] This requires that systems and processes are put in place to measure and manage how well organisations practise corporate governance and take steps to address performance gaps.[89] Regular performance evaluations are a fundamentally important part of this.

12.3. LEGISLATION IS INCREASING

Following a string of high-profile corporate failures in recent years, with corresponding losses of savings and jobs, there is an increasing focus on corporate governance. Many countries have introduced legislation to guide the process of governance and to ensure that boards of directors are fulfilling their governance responsibilities.[90] In many cases, the legislation has formalised the ways that directors are recruited, inducted, developed, evaluated and reappointed. It is no longer acceptable for boards to be "old boys' clubs" that are mere rubber stamps for the executive directors.

Many countries have introduced legislation to improve the quality of corporate governance in the public and private sectors. Examples of such countries are the following:

South Africa

The Code for Governance Principles for South Africa (referred to as "King IV") was introduced in 2017. One of the core principles of King IV is that the board should act as the focal point for, and custodian of, corporate governance. Unlike previous versions of the codes, King IV applies to all organisations, regardless of the manner or form of their establishment. As regards performance evaluation, King IV requires that annual evaluations of the board, its committees and directors (including evaluations of the chairperson, chief executive officer [CEO] and other executive directors) should be performed by the chairperson or an independent service provider. The overview of the process should be disclosed in the integrated report. The performance evaluation of directors assists in identifying their training needs and should be a requisite before reappointment. King IV's focus is thus on performance improvement, not just compliance.

The public sector (see section 51(1)(a)(i) of the Public Finance Management Act [PFMA]) requires that the accounting authority of a public entity "must ensure that the public entity has and maintains effective, efficient and transparent systems of financial and risk management and internal control". The National Treasury, in April 2010, issued the Public Sector Risk Management Framework in response to the requirements of the PFMA. This is consistent with the governance principles of King IV.

United Kingdom

The United Kingdom Corporate Governance Code states: "Individual evaluation should aim to show whether each director continues to contribute effectively and demonstrates commitment to the role (including commitment of time for the board and committee meetings and other duties). The chairman should act on the results of the performance evaluation by recognising the strengths and addressing the weaknesses of the board and, where appropriate, proposing new members to be appointed to the board or seeking the resignation of directors."

Board evaluation may be conducted internally. However, companies on the FTSE350 are required to conduct an external evaluation at least every three years.

United States of America

The Sarbanes-Oxley Act of 2002 (SOX) led the New York Stock Exchange (NYSE) to adopt listing standards stating that the boards of companies listed on the NYSE should conduct regular evaluations of their boards of directors to determine if their boards and committees are functioning properly. The NYSE also requires that the charters of the audit, nominating/ corporate governance and compensation committees of listed companies include provisions for an annual performance evaluation for such committees.

Some countries have adopted a "comply or explain" approach to corporate governance. Their requirements are principles-based and companies are expected to tailor them to fit their specific needs and situations. King III, on the other hand, prefers the term "apply or explain" because the word "comply" could denote a mindless response to the King Code and its recommendations, whereas the "apply or explain" regime shows an appreciation for the fact that it is often not a case of whether to comply or not, but rather to consider how the principles and recommendations can be applied. At the other end of the spectrum, the United States of America has chosen to codify a significant part of its governance in the Sarbanes-Oxley Act. This statutory regime is known as "comply or else". In other words, there are legal sanctions for noncompliance.

12.4. ADVANTAGES OF BOARD EVALUATIONS

Despite legislation in many countries, there are real business benefits to conducting regular board evaluations and acting on the results. Board evaluations, if conducted properly, can contribute significantly to performance improvements on three levels – organisational, board and individual director. Boards which commit to a regular evaluation process find benefits across these levels in terms of improved leadership, greater clarity of roles and responsibilities, improved teamwork, greater accountability, better decision making, improved communications, and more efficient board operations.

One of the key benefits of a board evaluation is that it can strengthen the board's leadership role, setting the tone and culture of the organisation. By adopting performance evaluation, the board provides an example for the CEO and senior managers to follow and demonstrates the values of the organisation. This lead-by-example role is essential for an organisation that is introducing or reinforcing performance management in the organisation. It clearly demonstrates that performance management starts at the top.

12.5. THE ROLE OF THE BOARD

Before a board can be evaluated, there needs to be a clear understanding amongst directors as to what the board is responsible for, and against what standards and measures it will be evaluated. All too often, however, there is lack of clarity amongst board members on these issues. This can be clearly seen in performance evaluations, where some directors rate an aspect of the board's performance as excellent, whereas others rate it as poor. Thus, before the performance of a board can be evaluated, it is essential for all directors to have the same understanding of what is required of the board so that they are all evaluating performance against a common standard. The United Kingdom's Corporate Governance Code defines the role of the board as follows:

Main principle

Every company should be headed by an effective board which is collectively responsible for the long-term success of the company.

Supporting principles

The board's role is to provide entrepreneurial leadership of the company within a framework of prudent and effective controls which enable risk to be assessed and managed. The board should set the company's strategic aims, ensure that the necessary financial and human resources are in place for the company to meet its objectives, and review management performance. The board should set the company's values and standards to ensure that its obligations to its shareholders and others are understood and met. All directors must act in the best interests of the company, consistent with their statutory duties.

From these broad principles, charters for the board and committees should be developed, as well as profiles for the individual roles such as the board and committee chairpersons, the CEO, directors and the company secretary. These charters and profiles should clearly specify what is required, and the standards of performance against which actual performance will be measured.

With this common understanding in place, it is a relatively straightforward matter to evaluate performance, identify performance gaps, and agree specific development actions to close these gaps.

12.6. FRAMEWORK FOR A BOARD EVALUATION

Many directors resist the idea of having their performance evaluated. They feel, having attained the level of director, that they have "made it" and it is unnecessary and even insulting to be subjected to performance evaluations. The first step is to demonstrate to directors that their own performance evaluation can lead to improvements in governance and sustainability for the organisation and sets an example for all other employees. The message should be that the focus of evaluations is development rather than just measurement. Directors should be involved in the design of the evaluation process and surveys to ensure their commitment and buy-in. Directors who are not committed to the process may well go through the motions of the evaluation, but this may contribute little to improving board performance.

Setting the parameters and scope of a board evaluation comprises a number of steps, as shown in Figure 12.1 below. Working systematically through each of these steps helps clarify the objectives of the evaluation and the mechanics and processes through which it will be conducted. Each of these steps is discussed in turn.

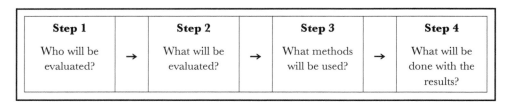

Step 1		Step 2		Step 3		Step 4
Who will be evaluated?	→	What will be evaluated?	→	What methods will be used?	→	What will be done with the results?

Figure 12.1: Steps in carrying out a board performance evaluation

12.6.1   Step 1: Who will be evaluated?

The requirement is that boards, committees and individual directors should be evaluated annually. However, depending on the board's experience in conducting performance evaluations, it may be advisable to start modestly and entrench the process rather than trying to do everything at once. As the directors become comfortable with the process, the scope of the evaluations can be expanded.

The first priority is to evaluate the performance of the board as a whole. This is the least threatening approach to evaluation because it focuses on group performance rather than individual director performance. Evaluating the board as a whole is appropriate when there are issues relating to board culture and differing perceptions of the board's roles and responsibilities. Board evaluations can be useful as a team-building exercise to develop a shared understanding of governance roles. Evaluating the performance of the whole board will usually identify weaknesses that can be linked to the performance of the committees and/or individual directors. Having established this in the first year, subsequent evaluations can cover these as well.

Board committees are an important governance mechanism, particularly in large companies. The members of these committees are usually specialists in a specific area, such as audit, remuneration, nominations, capital investment, and others. Committee evaluations typically cover two main areas: Is the charter of the committee clear and suited to the purpose of the committee? And how well does the committee perform in relation to its charter? Decisions taken in a committee usually have to be ratified by the board as a whole, but committees that function effectively can greatly enhance the overall performance of a board.

Board and committee performance is a function of the knowledge, skills and attitudes of the individual directors. Thus, companies should progress to evaluating the performance of individual directors as soon as they accept and are comfortable with the process of board evaluation. These can include the board chairperson, the CEO, committee chairpersons, individual directors and committee members. Very often, the company secretary is also evaluated. These are discussed below:

1. **Individual directors:** Evaluating the performance of individual directors can be beneficial if performance problems on the board relate to: skills gaps; the effectiveness of director recruitment processes; director induction; the ongoing development of individual directors; ethical concerns; the view that some directors are not pulling their weight; and difficult individuals who dominate board proceedings or are disruptive.

2. **The board chairperson:** The chairperson is pivotal in creating the conditions for overall board and director effectiveness, both inside and outside the boardroom. The chairperson has the responsibility of leading the board in setting the values and standards of the company and of maintaining a relationship of trust with and between the executive and non-executive members. Evaluating the chairperson is of fundamental importance to improving the overall effectiveness of the board.[91]

3. **The CEO:** The tasks of selecting the CEO and monitoring and evaluating his or her performance are key roles of a board. A comprehensive evaluation of the CEO helps to build a stronger relationship between the executives and the board and sets a valuable example throughout the organisation.

4. **The company secretary:** In terms of the Companies Act of 2008, public companies and state-owned enterprises are required to appoint a company secretary. Traditionally, company secretaries played a largely administrative role, for example by compiling and distributing board papers and taking minutes. However, company secretaries are increasingly being delegated a wide range of compliance responsibilities. The evaluation of the company secretary is key to an effective board.

12.6.2 Step 2: What will be evaluated?

The range and complexity of the issues facing a board and its directors have increased markedly in recent years. A successful evaluation depends on an understanding of the issues facing the board, identifying the root causes of problem areas, and coming up with feasible interventions for improvement.

Deciding on the scope of the evaluation is important. Ideally, boards need to understand the areas that, if improved, will make a substantial difference to overall board performance, rather than wasting time on things that do not really matter. Also, there are limits to the number of problem areas a board can try to fix simultaneously, and this makes it essential to prioritise. The framework below is a useful mechanism to help boards appreciate all the components of board performance that could potentially be evaluated, and then select those that will have the greatest impact. The question of what should be evaluated also depends on whether this is a first-time evaluation. If it is, a broad-based evaluation will help identify areas of concern. If evaluations have been undertaken previously, then the evaluation could focus on those areas that were previously identified for improvement.

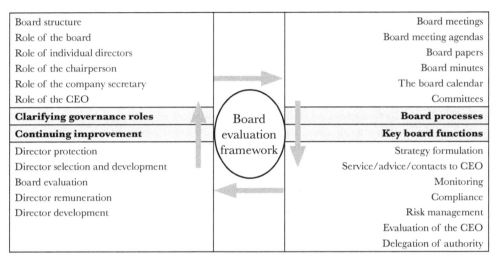

Figure 12.2: Board evaluation framework

The above framework shows that there are four essential elements of a high-performance board. These elements, along with illustrative evaluation questions, are as follows:

1   Roles:

    a. Is the board large enough to carry out the role required of it?

    b. Does the spread of talent within the board reflect the company's need?

2   Board processes:

    a. Are board members diligent in preparing for board meetings?

    b. Do the board papers contain the correct amount and type of information?

3   Functions:

    a. Is the board sufficiently involved in developing and approving the company's strategic plan?

    b. Does the company have reliable internal reporting and compliance systems?

4   Continuing improvement:

    a. Are there clear and well-understood policies and procedures in place for director selection and induction?

    b. Does the board encourage directors to pursue opportunities for personal development?

The elements of corporate governance are discussed below.

Clarifying governance roles

The first essential element is to clearly define and communicate the roles of the board, the committees and each individual. This will ensure that all individuals have a clear and common understanding of these roles. There should be a charter for the board and for each committee, and individual directors should have a letter of appointment clearly specifying their roles, responsibilities and time commitments. These charters and letters of appointment form the basis for future performance evaluations. In effect, they are the board's key performance areas.

A brief summary of the roles of the board as a whole, the chairperson and independent directors is given below:

1. **Role of the board:** Every company should be headed by an effective board which is collectively responsible for the long-term success of the company.

2. **Role of the chairperson:** The chairperson should demonstrate leadership abilities by setting an example to the rest of the board. He or she is responsible for setting the board's agenda and for ensuring that adequate time is available for discussion of all agenda items, in particular strategic issues. The chairperson should build a sound relationship with the CEO and promote a culture of openness and debate by facilitating the effective contribution of non-executive directors in particular, and ensuring constructive relations between executive and non-executive directors. The chairperson is responsible for ensuring that the directors receive accurate, timely and clear information. The chairperson should ensure effective communication with shareholders.

3. **Role of the non-executive directors:** Non-executive directors should approve the company's strategy, scrutinise the performance of management in meeting agreed goals and objectives, and monitor the reporting of performance. They should satisfy themselves on the integrity of financial information and that financial controls and systems of risk management are robust and defensible. They are responsible for determining appropriate levels of remuneration of executive directors and have a prime role in appointing and, where necessary, removing executive directors, and in succession planning.

Improving board processes

Once board members are comfortable in their roles, the focus turns towards productivity issues. Since board meetings are at the centre of the company's corporate governance processes, boards should evaluate, in the broader context, their effectiveness. This includes the quality, completeness and timeliness of board papers; the structure of the agenda to ensure that all key issues are covered in the time available; the quality and completeness of the board minutes; whether the annual calendar of board meetings, including special strategy meetings, is adequate to discharge the board's responsibilities effectively; and, finally, how well board meetings are run. This last point includes ensuring that board meetings are collegial and team-based, and that sufficient time is allowed for discussion of complex or contentious issues and for ensuring the participation of all members of the board.

Key board functions

The next step is to evaluate how effectively the board is carrying out the duties and functions defined in its charter. These include the formulation and approval of corporate strategy, monitoring performance, managing risk, and providing advice and counsel to the CEO and management team. A high-performance board will continuously assess how effectively these functions are carried out.

Continuing improvement

High-performance boards continuously strive to improve their performance and measure how effectively they are doing so.[92] Good governance requires that boards adopt and use formal processes for director recruitment, director induction, director development, and director evaluation and reappointment. The effectiveness of these processes should be monitored, as they are important drivers of board and director performance.

As this framework demonstrates, there are many areas where the effectiveness of the board and the directors can be evaluated – too many to work on feasibly at any one time. A company that is undertaking a board evaluation for the first time should undertake a broad-based evaluation to identify areas of weakness. In subsequent years, the focus can be on those areas that were previously highlighted for improvement.

Once the directors have accepted and are comfortable with the evaluation process, the organisation may then move on to evaluating the board committees, the committee chairpersons and members, and other roles such as the CEO and other executive directors and the company secretary.

Companies often use the same questionnaires for a period of time so they can track progress. Once these issues have been satisfactorily addressed, then other focus areas can be identified and performance monitored.

12.6.3   Step 3: What evaluation methods will be used?

Once it has been agreed who and what should be evaluated, the next step is to decide how the data should be collected. There are a number of different methods available, each requiring a different investment in time and administration. The choice is usually a balancing act between what is desirable and practicable. One also has to bear in mind the limited time availability of directors and their willingness to invest time in the process.

The chairperson of the board is ultimately responsible for board performance and should oversee the evaluation process. In some cases, the evaluations are carried out by the chairperson personally through group and/or one-on-one discussions with board members. Other companies make use of external service providers to conduct the evaluation process because this helps ensure impartiality and confidentiality. Other companies use a mix by conducting surveys themselves and using an external service provider to conduct follow-up analysis and interviews.

The choice of which methods to use is up to the company concerned. King IV does not specify any particular methodology, but notes that independent performance appraisals should be considered in the interest of eliciting candid responses. In the United Kingdom the listing requirements of the London Stock Exchange require FTSE350 companies to have the process conducted externally at least every three years. It is a requirement of both King IV and the United Kingdom Corporate Governance Code that a description of the evaluation process be included in the company's integrated report.

The process starts with the chairperson sending a communication to all directors, advising them of the process and how it will be conducted. It is noted that individual responses will remain confidential and that the intention is to identify areas where the performance of the board, committees and individual directors can be improved. The positive leadership of the chairperson is essential to the success of the initiative.

A 360-degree evaluation methodology is commonly used to obtain feedback from directors on the performance of the board as a whole, committees and individual directors. However, a 360-degree questionnaire on its own is of limited value because of the difficulty of interpreting the respondent's thoughts, or even if the respondent has fully understood the question. For this reason, most 360-degree surveys leave space for comments so that respondents can give reasons for their ratings and even propose solutions.

The value of a 360-degree survey is that it allows responses to be collected from multiple sources. For example, input can be requested from customers, suppliers and shareholders in addition to fellow board members. This is a major advantage over the chairperson conducting the evaluations through a one-on-one process. The 360-degree survey allows for quick analysis of what directors feel is right and wrong with board performance. It also allows the spread of responses to be observed, which may indicate that different directors have different perceptions of board performance.

The 360-degree questionnaires generally contain a number of statements that respondents are asked to rate on a scale ranging from "strongly agree" to "strongly disagree". For example, a typical statement may be: "Board pre-reading material is received in sufficient time to allow for adequate preparation." The advantage of respondents entering their responses directly onto a spreadsheet or online survey tool is that it enables quick consolidation and analysis of the results.

The 360-degree director questionnaires require that the respondent evaluates his or her own performance as well as getting the views of his or her peers. A comparison of these evaluations can reveal useful information such as "blind spots" or "hidden strengths". A blind spot is where the respondent's self-rating is more favourable than that of his or her peers, and a hidden strength is the opposite. This information helps tailor specific development opportunities for directors, and also helps identify areas of director strengths that the director may not have known he or she had.

Many companies further enhance the process by having the external service provider conduct interviews with respondents once the basic 360-degree questionnaires have been analysed. The service provider asks probing questions to understand why a respondent rated an item in a particular way. This helps ensure that respondents have the same understanding of the issue being rated, and also gives them the opportunity to propose solutions. Conducting interviews is obviously time-consuming, but the benefits can be substantial.

Another valuable way of obtaining information and recommendations, whilst simultaneously helping to build team spirit, is through group interviews. The key difference between this and individual interviews is that the interviewer takes on the role of moderator or facilitator, rather than that of interviewer. Instead of a question-and-answer process, the interviewer uses group dynamics to stimulate discussion of the key topics identified in the questionnaires.

Regardless of the methods used, it is important to emphasise that the output of the process is to identify areas for improvement. Once people understand this, they are more likely to admit their areas of weakness and accept the need for development. The chairperson's role in creating this positive atmosphere is key.

12.6.4 Step 4: What will be done with the results?

King IV states that "the performance evaluation of directors assists in identifying their training needs and should be a requisite before reappointment". Thus, the value of a performance evaluation is not so much in the results themselves, but in what is done with the results. The focus is thus on performance management rather than performance measurement.

The results of the board evaluation should be discussed with the full board in a special board meeting to ensure that directors take ownership of the process.[93] The board discussion can be led by the board chairperson or by an independent facilitator. All directors should be present and should be encouraged to contribute to the discussions, in particular those regarding the development actions to improve areas of weakness.[94] If carried out effectively, the process can help build a stronger and more cohesive team. The output of the discussions should be a prioritised list of development actions, with clear goals, time frames and responsibilities, in response to each performance gap.[95]

In a similar way, discussions in respect of each committee should be led by the committee chairperson or by an independent facilitator. Development priorities and development actions should be approved by the whole board prior to finalisation and implementation.

As regards performance feedback for individual directors[96], it is recommended that the board chairperson meets one on one with each director to discuss his or her performance, agree priorities and areas for development.[97] The non-executive directors, normally through the lead independent director, should provide feedback to the chairperson.

A development plan would typically specify the following:

1. What is to be accomplished? (the goal)
2. How is it to be accomplished? (a series of short-range objectives or actions)
3. What resources are needed? (funds, materials, staff)
4. Who is responsible? (chairperson, individual directors, company secretary)
5. When must the goal be completed? (a specific date, usually within a year)
6. How will accomplishment of the goal be measured? (follow-up survey results, client satisfaction, improved feedback)

12.7. SPECIMEN EVALUATION FORMS

The following specimen evaluation forms are provided as examples. They are generic in nature and should be tailored according to the specific requirements and circumstances of the company whose board and directors are being evaluated.

1. Evaluation of the board by all directors.
2. 360-degree evaluation of directors by self and colleagues. (Additional questions are provided to evaluate the chairperson.)

EVALUATION OF THE BOARD BY DIRECTORS							
Question number	Statement	Strongly agree	Agree	Slightly agree	Slightly disagree	Disagree	Strongly disagree
DEFINING GOVERNANCE ROLES							
BOARD PROCESSES							
KEY BOARD FUNCTIONS							
1	The board's mandate or terms of reference provides a clear and appropriate framework for the board's responsibilities						
2	The board has the appropriate number and types of committees in place						
3	The board calendar is well organised in terms of the number, timing and location of meetings						
4	The board actively guides the design of corporate governance in Company X and participates in its implementation						
5	The skills, knowledge and experience of board members are appropriate for Company X's needs						
6	There is a clear and well understood delineation between the roles of management and the board						
7	The board has succession plans in place for the Chairperson, CEO and individual directors and effectively oversees implementation of these plans						
8	Board pre-reading materials are received in sufficient time to allow for adequate preparation						
9	Board pre-reading materials provide the appropriate context and background information to support informed decision making						
10	Board meetings allow for candid, constructive discussion and critical questioning						
11	Board meetings provide sufficient opportunity for directors to seek and obtain input from management to support effective decision making						
12	Board meetings are appropriately focused on significant matters such as strategy, performance evaluation, risk assessment and governance						
13	Board meetings allow sufficient time to discuss the key issues						

EVALUATION OF THE BOARD BY DIRECTORS

Question number	Statement	Strongly agree	Agree	Slightly agree	Slightly disagree	Disagree	Strongly disagree
14	Directors receive appropriate information between meetings to keep abreast of significant issues, changes in legislation, trends and developments						
15	Board meetings allow sufficient time for committee feedback and discussion of issues raised by the board committees						
16	Directors are diligent in preparing for meetings						
17	Board meetings are conducted in a manner that ensures timely resolution of issues						
18	Directors have sufficient input into the organisation's strategic planning process and objectives and have signed off the appropriate documents						
19	Strategic plans presented to the board are reviewed regularly						
20	The board has established and continually monitors an appropriate number of financial and non-financial performance indicators						
21	The types of financial and non-financial reports received by the board are adequate for it to discharge its governance duties						
22	The board reviews and adopts an annual capital budget and receives regular reports of performance against the budget throughout the year						
23	The processes for monitoring and evaluating the CEO's and management's performance are satisfactory						
24	Directors have identified and documented appropriate risk mitigation measures and monitor performance against these measures						
25	Directors ensure that there is an effective risk-based internal audit function in the organisation						
26	Directors receive written assessments of the effectiveness of the organisation's system of internal controls and risk management						
27	Directors and management have identified the Company X's key stakeholders that impact on, or influence, Company X's long term sustainability						
28	Directors and management engage sufficiently with these stakeholders and have identified the issues that are important to them						

EVALUATION OF THE BOARD BY DIRECTORS

Question number	Statement	Strongly agree	Agree	Slightly agree	Slightly disagree	Disagree	Strongly disagree
29	Directors and management have a good understanding of, and comply with, the principles of integrated reporting, as required by King III						
30	The board has a working understanding of the effect of the applicable laws, rules, codes and standards on the organisation and its business						

CONTINUING DEVELOPMENT

Question number	Statement	Strongly agree	Agree	Slightly agree	Slightly disagree	Disagree	Strongly disagree
31	The process for identifying, assessing and appointing new directors is sufficiently rigorous						
32	The board orientation programme provides directors with appropriate information on their roles, responsibilities and duties						
33	There is sufficient emphasis on developing the capacity of directors to effectively perform their duties						
34	Directors are encouraged to continue in professional development to enhance their performance as directors						
35	There is a formal process in place to evaluate the performance of the board, committees, chairpersons and individual directors						

EVALUATION OF IHE BOARD BY DIRECTORS–ADDITIONAL COMMENTS

Please list your suggested changes or improvements to the structure or functioning of the board in the following areas:

Governance roles:

Board processes:

Board functions:

Continuing development:

Question number	Statement	Chairman (as director)						Director 2						Director 3						Director 4					
		Strongly disagree	Disagree	Slightly disagree	Slightly agree	Agree	Strongly agree	Strongly disagree	Disagree	Slightly disagree	Slightly agree	Agree	Strongly agree	Strongly disagree	Disagree	Slightly disagree	Slightly agree	Agree	Strongly agree	Strongly disagree	Disagree	Slightly disagree	Slightly agree	Agree	Strongly agree
KNOWLEDGE AND SKILLS																									
1	Has the necessary skills to contribute to the effective functioning of the board																								
2	Has a satisfactory understanding of Company X's business and long term strategic interests																								
3	Understands and demonstrates commitment to good corporate governance																								
4	Has a clear understanding of distinct roles of directors and managers																								
5	Understands his/her responsibilities and liabilities as a director																								
EXECUTION OF DUTIES																									
6	Contributes to the development of strategy and key performance measures for Company X																								
7	Contributes to the measurement of RW's performance and proposes corrective actions where necessary																								
8	Has a clear understanding of the risks and opportunities facing Company X and acts accordingly																								
9	Consults with management, customers, external advisors and other stakeholders as necessary																								
10	Acts in the best interests of Company X at all times and effectively manages conflicts of interests																								
11	Has a good understanding of Company X's operations and finances and contributes effectively																								

Question number	Statement	Chairman (as director)						Director 2						Director 3						Director 4					
		Strongly disagree	Disagree	Slightly disagree	Slightly agree	Agree	Strongly agree	Strongly disagree	Disagree	Slightly disagree	Slightly agree	Agree	Strongly agree	Strongly disagree	Disagree	Slightly disagree	Slightly agree	Agree	Strongly agree	Strongly disagree	Disagree	Slightly disagree	Slightly agree	Agree	Strongly agree
BOARD CONTRIBUTION																									
12	Forms and maintains effective working relationships with colleagues, management and other stakeholders																								
13	Devotes sufficient time to his/her directorial duties both during and outside formal meetings																								
14	Is consistently prepared and briefed for all matters to be discussed at meetings																								
15	Listens attentively to others and is respectful of their opinions and points of view																								
16	Willingly and openly shares relevant information																								
17	Contributes effectively to all board processes and discussions																								
DEVELOPMENT																									
18	Keeps up to date with key developments requiring his/her skills set																								
19	Keeps abreast relevant legislation and applies these in his/her duties																								
20	Seeks ways and takes action to improve his/her effectiveness as a director																								
21	Undertakes personal performance evaluation as a director and openly shares this with colleagues																								

STRENGTHS AND AREAS FOR IMPROVEMENT

For each person (including self), please list a maximum of three strengths and three areas for improvement

	Chairman (as director)	Director 2	Director 3	Director 4
1	Strength 1			
2	Strength 2			
3	Strength 3			
4	Area for improvement 1			
5	Area for improvement 2			
6	Area for improvement 3			

PLEASE ANSWER THE FOLLOWING ADDITIONAL QUESTIONS ON THE CHAIRPERSON		Strongly agree	Agree	Slightly agree	Slightly disagree	Disagree	Strongly disagree
1	Provides the necessary direction and leadership for an effective board						
2	Identifies and participates in selecting board members and oversees board succession planning						
3	Formulates, communicates and oversees an annual workplan for the board						
4	Works with CEO, company secretary and board members to develop effective meeting agendas						
5	Presides over board meetings and ensures that time is used effectively						
6	Ensures that presentations and discussions keep to the point and to the time allotted for them						
7	Acts as a link between the board and management, especially the CEO						
8	Ensures that all directors play a full and constructive role in the affairs of the company						
9	Ensures that each director's performance is evaluated annually and developed as required						

CHAIRPERSON'S STRENGTHS AND AREAS FOR IMPROVEMENT

For chairperson, please list a maximum of three strengths and three areas for improvement

Strength 1

Strength 2

Strength 3

Area for improvement 1

Area for improvement 2

Area for improvement 3

12.8. CONCLUSION

The global economy is going through a difficult period. At times of such challenge, it is even more critical than normal that boards of directors can plan effectively and take tough and strategic decisions – this requires proper board procedures in place, with all directors fully understanding their role and having the special skills that directors need. Good governance requires that the performance of the board is evaluated and that the evaluation process is a constructive mechanism for improving board effectiveness, maximising strengths and tackling weaknesses. Organisations that do not conduct rigorous board evaluations place themselves at risk of poor corporate governance as well as poor performance.

12.9. BIBLIOGRAPHY

Bennis, W. 2000. *Old dogs new tricks*. London: Kogan Page.

Block, P. 1993. *Stewardship*. San Francisco: Berrett-Koehler.

Ciulla, JB. 2003. *The ethics of leadership*. Belmont: Wadsworth.

Clemens, JK & Albrecht, S. 1995. *The timeless leader*. Holbrook, Massachusetts: Adams.

Corporate Research Foundation. 2002. *South Africa's leading managers 2003*. Cape Town: Corporate Research Foundation.

Corporate Research Foundation. 2004. *South Africa's leading managers 2004*. Cape Town: Corporate Research Foundation.

Covey, S. 1991. *Principle-centered leadership*. London: Simon & Schuster.

Diehl, D & Donnelly, MP. 2002. *How did they manage?* London: Spiro.

Garratt, B. 1996. *The fish rots from the head*. London: Harper Collins.

Garratt, B. 2003. *Thin on top*. Yarmouth: Nicholas Brealey.

Halpern, BL & Lubar, K. 2003. *Leadership presence*. New York: Gotham.

Harvard Business Review. 2000. Interviews with CEOs. Boston: Harvard Business School.

Haudan, J. 2008. *The art of engagement*. New York: McGraw-Hill.

Kakabadse, NK & Kakabadse, AP. 2007. Chairman of the board: demographics effects on role pursuit. *Journal of Management Development* 26(2):169-192.

Kellerman, B. 2004. *Bad leadership*. Boston: Harvard Business School.

Kets de Vries, MFR & Miller, D. 1987. *Unstable at the top*. New York: Mentor.

Kets de Vries, MFR. 1989. *Prisoners of leadership*. New York: John Wiley & Sons.

Kets de Vries, MFR. 2001. *The leadership mystique*. New York: Financial Times Prentice-Hall.

Khoza, RJ & Adam, M. 2005. *The power of governance*. Hyde Park & Rivonia: Pan MacMillan & Business in Africa (credited as an Eskom copyright).

Koestenbaum, P. 1991. *Leadership: the inner side of greatness*. San Francisco: Jossey-Bass.

Laborde, GZ. 1984. *Influencing with integrity*. San Francisco: Syntony.

Lennick, D & Kiel, F. 2005. *Moral intelligence*. Upper Saddle River: Wharton.

Mangeu, X. (ed) 2006. *The meaning of Mandela*. Cape Town. HSRC Press.

Nair, K. 1994. *A higher standard of leadership*. San Francisco: Berrett-Koehler.

Whicker, ML. 1996. *Toxic leaders*. Westport: Quorum Books.

Endnotes

83.   Bennis, 2000.
84.   Kellerman, 2004; Whicker, 1996.
85.   Harvard Business Review, 2000.
86.   Garratt, 1996; Garratt, 2003; Kets de Vries & Miller, 1987; Kets de Vries, 1989; Kets de Vries, 2001.
87.   Lennick & Kiel, 2005.
88.   Corporate Research Foundation, 2002; Corporate Research Foundation, 2004.
89.   Diehl & Donnelly, 2002.
90.   Khoza & Adam, 2005.
91.   Kakabadse & Kakabadse, 2007.
92.   Clemens & Albrecht, 1995.
93.   Block, 1993; Haudan, 2008.
94.   Koestenbaum 1991.
95.   Mangeu, 2006; Nair, 1994.
96.   Ciulla, 2003; Laborde, 1984.
97.   Covey, 1991.

13 DOES PERFORMANCE MANAGEMENT WORK?

13.1. INTRODUCTION

Theoretically, performance management processes are associated with performance improvement. Research has established that there is a high correlation between performance culture and performance management practices on the one hand, and business performance on the other.[98] Thus, empirically, there is a strong correlation between performance management and performance improvement. Why, then, are so many learned scholars and practitioners sceptical about the relationship? In this chapter, we will explore why.

13.2. THE PERFORMANCE MANAGEMENT PROCESS

The **mechanics** of the performance management process allow one to set targets, to evaluate performance against the targets, and to take corrective action if needed. It is then followed by appropriate consequences. Theoretically, performance should improve if the objectives are made clear to people. It is in the nature of humans to do the right thing. People will increase their performance if they know what is expected, how to do it and what the standards are. Under normal circumstances, people's survival instincts make them want to exceed targets.

If one provides feedback on performance, performance should improve further. People are competitive beings and their natural reaction will be to achieve or exceed targets. To perform better, people will welcome guidance to improve their performance. It is in their nature to optimise support to improve their performance. Finally, if there are positive consequences following on their performance, motivation levels will go up because they want to continue receiving positive reinforcement, and, similarly, if the consequences are negative, they will want to avoid the pain. Why, then, is this theoretical model not consistently true in relation to business performance?

To understand the problem, we should start by analysing the various elements of the **mechanics** of the performance management process and the sequence in which it should theoretically enhance performance. In Figure 13.1. below, the process of performance management is depicted graphically.

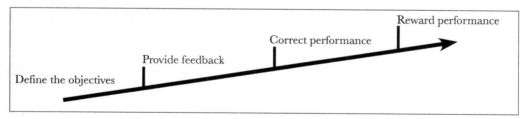

Figure 13.1: The sequential steps in performance management

In Fig 13.1 above, the vertical rules need to be tidied up such that they are all touching the thick oblique rule but not hanging above it or intersecting it.

Should the supervisor reverse the sequence, the effect on performance may be negatively affected. For example, if the manager starts off by emphasising the positive reward of performance without ensuring that there are standards and assessments, people will develop a culture of entitlement. The next time they will expect a positive reward without making any effort to improve performance. Similarly, if the standards are poorly defined and/or measured, a culture of entitlement will flourish. If the supervisor begins with an emphasis on negative enforcement, a culture of suspicion and conflict will result.

If we continue to reverse the sequence, the supervisor will find that, trying to correct performance without defining what is needed and assessing what was delivered, will be very difficult, and that employees will rebel against any "criticism" of their performance. Similarly, trying to give feedback when the objectives are not defined will be seen as baseless and without appreciation of the situation in which the employee finds himself or herself.

> The learning from this is that the performance management process is systematic. One cannot miss one step in the process and expect to achieve sustained, improved performance. The same happens if one of the steps is not done effectively – for example, if the objectives are not defined well, the rest of the process is flawed.

13.3. SETTING OBJECTIVES

The Corporate Leadership Council[99] found that avoiding risk is the second-most important reason why performance management fails. The more pressure that is placed on performance, the more employees negotiate easier targets. "Streetwise" employees also negotiate easy targets. This is made worse where the employer rewards performance. Streetwise employees earn larger bonuses and, to make matters worse, the rest of the employees observe this and committed employees become risk avoiders because they feel cheated and also want to earn big bonuses.

The negotiation of soft targets is euphemistically referred to as "fat in the budget", a "bottom-up budget", an "inflation-adjusted budget", et cetera. This often happens if there is insufficient **attention to detail** on the part of managers, especially if the manager does not verify targets below direct reports. In order to overcome these limitations, an elaborate process of target negotiation should take place.

As part of the target-setting process, managers should not only consider in-house factors, but should also use external benchmarks and ensure that the business remains competitive. Care should be taken that the targets are not pulling the company down to the average, but rather pushing it up.

There are a myriad of different theoretical models on performance target-setting: key performance indicators (KPIs); key result areas (KRAs); balanced scorecards; strategic initiatives; et cetera. If ever the accusation that theoretical models are used to justify a situation were true, it would certainly apply to performance management. It often happens that a chosen model is forced to fit into an organisation, and theoretical objectives are created because the model "requires" it. In these cases, people experience target-setting as merely theoretical and the process loses credibility.

While understanding the need for structure in performance management, the tail should never wag the dog. This is potentially a difficult decision for the designers, because a lack of structure is equally ineffective. Somewhere, an optimum design point should be found, as depicted in Figure 13.2. below.

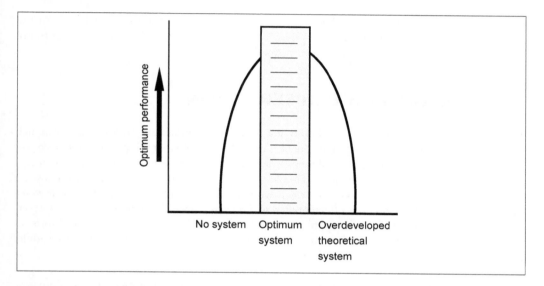

Figure 13.2: Finding an optimum design for the performance management system

13.4. THE DYNAMICS OF OBJECTIVE-SETTING

Thus far, this chapter has only focused on the **mechanics** of the process. There are also the **dynamics** of the process. These dynamics refer to the values and the "how" of the process. Too often, target-setting is a mechanistic process and not a challenge to deliver exceptional results. In sport, athletes/players are challenged to exceed their own expectations, and they often do. Why do athletes/players succeed?

Not all athletes/players succeed. The ones who do are better prepared, probably more skilled (but not necessarily so), and believe that they are the best. The same applies to business. Performance management that exists in isolation has no relevance. Performance management may optimise performance if the mechanics are implemented correctly; however, if the **efficacy** does not exist, the means for performance are not available, and stumbling blocks in performance are not removed, the process becomes academic. Before any performance management process is implemented, an assessment of the organisation's readiness for the implementation should be conducted.

The issue of target-setting and the credibility of targets are the subject of constant debate. This happens because of a lack of governance guidelines. The board of the company should set the tone by defining the risk–return ratio. Shareholders should know that, if they want higher returns, the risk will increase. If management is expected to gamble, the risk of losing increases.

Therefore, the resources, risk mitigation and consequence management should be related (even if the consequence means forgiveness). No system is immune to a lack of discretion. Managerial art applies to performance management, and sensitising managers to these softer "dynamics" should form part of the implementation of the performance management system.

A mechanical solution of target calibration, where targets and objectives are rolled up in the organisation, is recommended, provided that it is not turned into a bureaucratic nightmare riddled with inefficiencies and character assassination.

13.5. PERFORMANCE OBSERVATION

The Corporate Leadership Council[100] found that the key determinant of success in performance management is timeous (on-the-spot) feedback – regardless of whether it is positive or corrective. This just-in-time feedback is a powerful motivator, an assurance to the employee, and a systematic guide to success. In practice, it is not so simple. Managers are often removed from employees, and performance reviews only take place once every few months. This is exacerbated by the fact that performance management is often equated to a review or examination, which the employee has to pass, and for which he or she must submit a "body of evidence". This leads to all sorts of counterproductive behaviour. Performance management in its most natural environment should take place on the job and in a coaching relationship.

Performance management that is based on assumed observation is not credible and damages the employment relationship. It is better not to do performance management than to assume that the supervisor has observed performance. If employees cannot trust their supervisor with sensitive assessments such as their performance, trust in many other areas is lost. Performance management designers are aware of this problem and have introduced various solutions. The development of "output" models is an example of a design where supervisors can "wash their hands", because they only have to measure the output and not the input. How people achieve the results does not matter until conflict in values and cooperation problems appear. These models also remove the opportunity for the supervisor to get involved in the performance obstacles of the employee. In sport, the better coaches are involved in smoothing out the performance obstacles of the sportsperson, and this is how they grow.

A further technique developed is the 360-degree feedback mechanism where peers, subordinates, managers and customers are used to evaluate performance. These techniques are difficult to administer and are often manipulated, which is damaging to relationships, trust and the status of performance culture in the organisation. External feedback has a place in performance management, but, unless the information is reliable and relevant, it can be more damaging to the cause.

Performance observation is a challenge. It is also a reflection of the supervisor's managerial and leadership skills. The better supervisors have time to consult with their direct reports, and to be involved in their performance obstacles and achievements.

13.6. PERFORMANCE ASSESSMENT

The interpersonal skills necessary to set objectives and to give feedback are well documented and seem to be the basic skills that most organisations are able to embed. However, performance management systems are burdened with many deliverables. These requirements increase the risks to a sound performance management process.

In addition, it is important to consider the impact of performance management on the employees themselves. To the individual, there is an ego challenge, the fear of losing employment, the link to remuneration, and the anxiety of potentially not being included in the "in-group" of high performers. One can easily understand why this process is filled with emotional stress. To make matters worse, a large proportion of people supervising others should never be placed in a position to manage people. Job competence is far too often equated with the ability to manage and lead staff.

Performance management process designers have responded to many of the flaws in performance feedback. For example, to overcome the problem of having too many top performers, forced distributions were introduced. In a forced distribution, a normal distribution curve is imposed where set quotas for top performers are enforced. A normal distribution for performance is statistically unfounded and is a good example of enforcing a theoretical model on reality. Implementing scientifically indefensible practices has lowered trust levels and discredits performance management.

Auditing of performance assessments via moderation committees has become widespread. The intention of these committees is honourable; however, the application of the process is riddled with flaws. Managers who use these platforms to negotiate on behalf of their own staff and ignore the larger group create a dysfunctional competitive environment. The effect is time-consuming, involving frivolous meetings with a profound impact on morale, trust and, ultimately, culture. There is evidence that these models can work. The common theme in successful moderation processes is authentic leadership, involvement from the senior level down, and a clear set of governance rules by the leader which are agreed to and supported by the members of the panel. Leaders need to deal with any suspicion of hidden agendas (in these moderation panels) in no uncertain terms.

It seems that the solution to effective performance assessment lies in the **dynamics** of the process rather than the mechanistic procedures. It lies in the authenticity of the collective leadership, the values and commitment to excellence towards staff, and their expectations of the employment relationship. Performance management is arguably one of the most sensitive people processes that a supervisor should manage, and it requires skills and good governance. Most organisations look at the mechanistic aspects of the process and underestimate the complexity of the dynamics of the interpersonal and intrapersonal relationships.

13.7. CONSEQUENCE MANAGEMENT

Performance management without consequences is irrelevant. There must be consequences for performance or lack thereof. The wider the application of the consequences, the more productive supervisory time becomes. It potentially should support the performance culture in the organisation.

With modern information technology, there is a tendency to create a "hard" or direct link between performance assessment and other business processes. This ignores the fact that management is equally an art and a science. Skilful supervisors (leaders) are limited by these systems. Their coaching and personal style to motivate and engage with their direct reports is inhibited by rigid systems. However, the persistent authentic leader will find ways around this and reduce proper analytical procedures to the mechanistic codes required by system designers. The problem remains that the majority of supervisors treat performance management as an administrative process where boxes need to be ticked, and deem their job done when the paperwork is completed.

When the consequences of performance become irrelevant, the poor performers become entitled to not having to perform and good performers become disillusioned with the hypocrisy of the system. Both are terminal to the performance culture and the courageous thing to do is to remove, or fundamentally change, the performance management system. This requires committed management, governance, attention to detail, and skilful leadership.

Performance management often requires too much policing. Managers are not naturally inclined to participate. They sometimes avoid it because the feedback is negative and requires that they hold tough conversations which are uncomfortable. Performance management is also seen as extra work and not a natural process of leadership. Skills are often lacking and governance of performance management in most cases is non-existent. A policy that sets out activities and administrative procedures provides some form of governance. However, the spirit of performance improvement, of authentically engaging with employees, is a higher order of role modelling and it seems to be at the root of poor performance management practices. There seems to be a high correlation between the presence of a strong performance culture and performance management. However, the direction of the correlation is not performance management first, but the other way round. Performance culture and performance leadership come first.

13.8. READINESS ASSESSMENT FOR PERFORMANCE MANAGEMENT

A practical method to navigate all the risks and challenges of performance management is to conduct a readiness assessment before the performance management system is implemented. Such a readiness assessment could also be done in organisations where a performance management system is already in operation. The purpose of the readiness assessment is to determine if the organisation is ready for performance management, and whether it will benefit from it. The benefits of doing the assessment are obvious:

- no loss of credibility as a result of implementing a failed system
- an opportunity to determine what is preventing success, and to implement steps to prepare the organisation

- assessment of the probability of success
- a better-guided implementation plan

The above also applies to "auditing" existing performance management systems. The value lies in the improvement (even removal) of ineffective systems that poison the performance culture. The continued use of a performance management system that does not work is harmful to the organisation.

Readiness assessments or audits of existing performance management systems and practices should be done with empirically validated instruments. The home-made, family magazine-type questionnaire will probably give the answer the designer wants – not a reliable and defensible assessment. It is also better to use objective assessments and benchmarks that are standardised for comparable organisations.

There is no point in doing the assessments if there will not be corrective action. In the case of readiness assessments, the purpose of the assessment is to prepare the organisation. Sometimes, it will require major change management procedures. The same applies where an existing performance management system is "audited". The change interventions will, in most cases, indicate some form of governance, leadership role and interpersonal skills development. Be prepared for it.

13.9. CONCLUSION

There is no doubt that performance management can work and can lead to increased and sustained high performance. The determinants of success, however, are numerous and complex. A performance management system that is not well designed and implemented can be counterproductive. The tools and processes are important components of performance management, but the philosophy behind the system and management efficacy in driving the system are key levers of success. Performance management cannot be implemented as a tick-box exercise and be expected to drive a legitimate high-performance culture.

13.10. BIBLIOGRAPHY

Corporate Leadership Council. April 2011. *Performance management – survey findings*.

De Swardt, L. 2005. The development and validation of a variable remuneration methodology, Unpublished PhD Thesis, University of Johannesburg.

Endnotes

98.   De Swardt 2005.
99.   The Corporate Leadership Council, 2011.
100.   The Corporate Leadership Council, 2011.

14 CRITICAL SUCCESS FACTORS AND TRENDS

Performance management is and will always be an integral part of every business. Every manager and business owner without exception, with or without formal training, practises performance management on an intuitive level every day. They may not even know it is called "performance management", but it is permanently on their mind – how to increase the effectiveness of the company by improving the performance of the people who work in it.

No matter what else changes around them, there are a few factors that will never change. Organisational leaders will always want:

1. To improve organisational performance
2. To align individual and organisational objectives
3. To align individual behaviour with values of the organisation
4. To provide the basis of personal development
5. To develop a performance culture
6. To improve individual performance
7. To confirm contribution/performance pay decision
8. To motivate people

This is where performance management comes in.

Performance is obviously an extremely difficult variable to measure, especially in today's rapidly changing organisations. Results and measures become obsolete very quickly, and translating interactions and human desires to measurements may be seen as unlikely and impersonal. This means that a PM system has to be continually evaluated against its goals.

We need to conduct more empirical research on why some organisations get performance management right and some do not. They use the same forms, refer to the same books and use the same consultants. Here are five possible reasons and critical success factors that, in my experience, make some systems work and others not.

1. **The chief executive officer (CEO) owns performance management in the organisation**

   I have personally worked in an organisation were the CEO wanted to know if executives held their performance reviews with subordinates and explained the goals and strategies of the organisation. If not, they got zero pay increases and zero bonuses. Executives were also not allowed to cancel performance appraisal appointments more than once.

2. **A clear understanding of corporate strategy**

   Everyone understands the goals and strategy of the organisation, their division and department and how what they do supports this.

3. **Simple documentation**

Long and elaborate documentation and performance appraisal forms are often confusing. My personal favourite form is a blank piece of paper which I write on in front of the person I am appraising:

o   **Start** – I want you to start doing these things.

o   **Stop** – I want you to stop doing these things.

o   **Continue** – Please continue to do the following; you are doing them well.

4. **A conversation takes place**

The emphasis is on having a decent conversation. It seeks to understand, is nurturing, is solution-oriented and it builds. It builds confidence, and it builds on current good work that is being done.

5. **An output-oriented culture**

One of the most profound "step changes" that an organisation can make in the performance management arena is embracing the concept of "outputs, not activities". It changes the way one thinks about work, about what needs to be done and about how it should be done.

I believe that it is the most effective, humane and efficient method of performance management that actually aligns thinking from the bottom to the top. It allows for a full appreciation of the entire value chain and drives the organisation strategy.

Companies need to stop spending money on new IT systems, step back and take a more strategic and holistic approach. The company's most important metrics need to be identified in order to help build an organisational system that will translate the data into actionable business insights and more useful decision making.

On a practical level, changes that companies can make to modernise their systems include:

1. Simpler forms
2. Abolishing two rating sessions a year and replacing them with ongoing conversations
3. Removing forced ranking
4. Avoiding moderating performance scores at the expense of line manager authority

Whether or not it is in a formal programme, performance management will always be part and parcel of every organisation. It is a tool that can be used to great advantage, if only harnessed to the right horses. Simply put, performance management systems need to get more intelligent.

The key trends in PM can be summarised as follows:

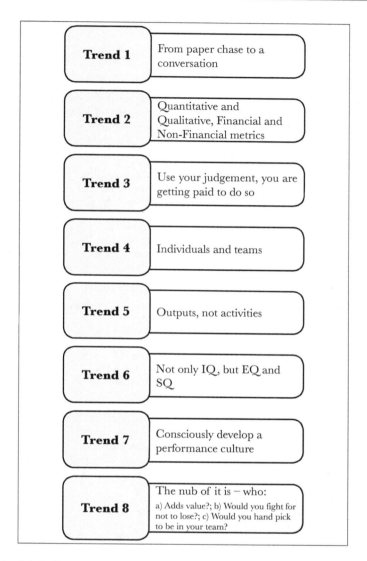

Trend 1	From paper chase to a conversation
Trend 2	Quantitative and Qualitative, Financial and Non-Financial metrics
Trend 3	Use your judgement, you are getting paid to do so
Trend 4	Individuals and teams
Trend 5	Outputs, not activities
Trend 6	Not only IQ, but EQ and SQ
Trend 7	Consciously develop a performance culture
Trend 8	The nub of it is – who: a) Adds value?; b) Would you fight for not to lose?; c) Would you hand pick to be in your team?

Figure 14.1: Key trends in performance management

Whether or not it is in a formal programme, performance management will always be part and parcel of every organisation. It is a tool that can be used to great advantage, if only harnessed to the right horses. Simply put, performance management systems need to get more intelligent.

I would like to hear your views on performance management, especially success stories that we could include as a case study in future versions of this book. Please e-mail me on drbussin@mweb.co.za.

I look forward to your contributions.

Index

[Created with **TExtract** / www.Texyz.com]

Lightning Source UK Ltd.
Milton Keynes UK
UKHW030220161022
410543UK00007B/202